WITH PIPE, PADDLE, AND SONG

ALSO BY ELIZABETH YATES

Amos Fortune, Free Man
Mountain Born
A Place for Peter
The Next Fine Day
The Journeyman
Hue and Cry
Prudence Crandall, Woman of Courage
Someday You'll Write
Sound Friendships

With Pipe, Paddle, and Song

A Story of the French-Canadian Voyageurs

by Elizabeth Yates

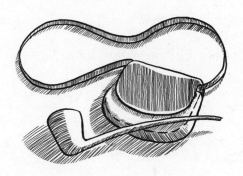

BETHLEHEM BOOKS • IGNATIUS PRESS
Bathgate   San Francisco

The songs on pages 227, 230, 232, 238, 245, 247, and 253 are from *Jongleur Songs of Old Quebec* by Marius Barbeau.

The songs on pages 223, 234, 240, 242, 249 and 251 are from *Folk Songs of French Canada* by Marius Barbeau and Edward Sapir.

The author wishes to thank John Parker, Curator of the James Ford Bell Collection at the University of Minnesota, who read the book in manuscript and offered several valuable suggestions.

The publishers would like to thank Deloris Kanten for her support in the production of the current edition.

Revised Bethlehem Books Edition 1998

ISBN 978-1-883937-37-9
Library of Congress Catalog Number: 98-73486

Bethlehem Books • Ignatius Press
10194 Garfield Street S, Bathgate ND 58216

Printed in the United States on acid free paper

WITH PIPE, PADDLE, AND SONG

Note

Some of the voyageur songs mentioned in the story can be found set to music with lyrics in French and English in a section beginning on page 223. The following songs are included:

En Roulant Ma Boule
Le Coeur de Ma Bien-aimée
Le Bâtiment Merveilleux
Alouette!
Le Miracle du Nouveau-Né
Il S'est Mis à Turlutter
À Saint-Malo
L'Hirondelle, Messagère de l'Amour
C'est l'Aviron Qui Nous Mène
Je Sais Bien Quelque Chose
Cette Aimable Tourterelle
Je ne Suis Pas Si Vilaine
L'Herbe Verdit Tous les Printemps

Height of Land
Portage

Pigeon R.

Grand Portage
[The Great Lake]
LAKE SUPERIOR

The First Two Thousand Miles
of
THE GREAT TRACE

LAKE
MICHIGAN

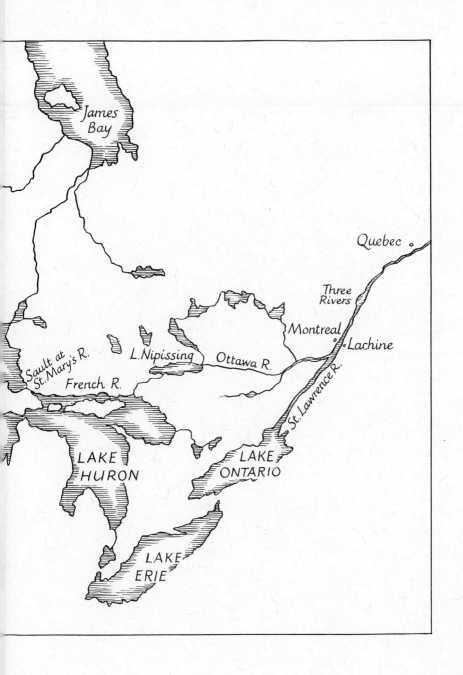

Chapter One

GUILLAUME PUISSANTE stood on the wharf and watched the wind fill the sails of the great ship as she headed her prow east and into the widening river, into the wider ocean, and so to France. France! He knew the land as he knew the back of his hand, but in all his sixteen years he had not seen it; and though he might live to be many times sixteen he doubted that he would ever see it.

As long as the small group of people remained on the deck waving, he would stand on the wharf. Even when he could see the people no longer, he would still stand there. He would leave only when the white sails disappeared into the broad blue beyond and the tie that held him to *Le Cygne Chantant* had snapped.

"Adieu, Monsieur le Comte!" He shouted into the wind. He could not say "À bientôt" or even "Au revoir"; he could only wish well to the journey. "Bon voyage, Monsieur le Comte!"

The wind that whipped around him carried an echo of Monsieur le Comte's farewell words: "Allons, mon grand; we must go forward. It is the only place to go."

Guillaume shivered, partly from the chilling lash of the

wind but more from pride as he recalled the time when
Monsieur le Comte had first called him "mon grand."

He had always known there would be a time when
Monsieur le Comte would return to France. That was the
way of life in New France. Chevaliers and soldiers, men of
business and profession, adventurers, came to live in the
New World for a while; sometimes their ladies came with
them, and they remained long enough to establish their
families; but for most of them, their ladies and families
remained on the far side of the ocean and were rejoined
after a few years of service or business had been accomplished in Montréal or Québec or one of the smaller
settlements.

The ice had moved out of the river early in that spring
of 1750; and when the first news came with the first ship,
it had been received with grave concern. "I fear for New
France," Monsieur le Comte had said to Guillaume. "There
are strange things happening in the world, and we may
not be able to hold our position here for many more years,
and there is so much wealth." He told Guillaume that he
had been recalled by the King and that he could not be
sorry. He had been away from the court for a long time
and he would be glad to live again as a Frenchman in
France.

Guillaume's dark eyes, fixed upon Monsieur le Comte's
face, were filled with wonder. On his lips trembled a
question he dared not ask.

Monsieur le Comte said: "When *Le Cygne Chantant* is
loaded with furs for the markets in Europe, and sets sail
again, I shall go with her. You are a man now, Guillaume;
you will find your own work."

The expression in the dark eyes turned to sadness.

"You are strong, you are clever, you are brave, Guillaume," Monsieur le Comte went on, accenting his words carefully; "there are fortunes still to be made in New France by young men such as you. Only remember, Guillaume, that you are French, and enjoy what you have and do. It is a mistake to work only for a tomorrow that may never come."

"Mais oui, Monsieur le Comte."

"Perhaps, someday, we shall meet—" and there the words stopped.

Guillaume found it hard to reply. When he could trust himself to speak, he could not trust himself to look into Monsieur le Comte's face so he turned his head away and said, "Not someday, Monsieur le Comte, but in heaven."

The mere utterance of the words gave Guillaume confidence and fanned the flame of pride that burned within him. Free now to face the future without commitment or promise, he turned to face Monsieur le Comte, and smiled up at him. So doing, he made himself available to the older man's benison: a kiss, first on the left cheek, then on the right. After bestowing it, Monsieur le Comte laughed as if a game had been played at which each had won. Then he asked Guillaume to pour a glass of wine for him and sing to him.

Not one song but many were sung, and with them Guillaume felt more sure of the life that was before him, and eager to pursue it.

Standing alone on the wharf and waiting for the ship to disappear, he remembered that night. Only the white sails could be seen now, and they were mere tips on the distant blue. The wind was serving *Le Cygne Chantant*. The first day of her long journey was going well. Guillaume started to sing aloud one of the songs Monsieur le Comte had taught him, the one about the swallow who was the messenger of love. By the time he came to the end of the seventh verse, the end of the song, the sails had disappeared.

He watched the river, its surface ruffled by the wind. The sun that wrapped him in its light was warm, warm enough to release the pungent fragrance of pitch from the pines along the river, warm enough to turn into rivulets the few remaining snowbanks; but the wind was sharp, and its edge would be even keener by sundown. When night came, winter's legacy of cold would still be apparent. But word had come down from the pays d'en haut—the upper country, the wilderness—that rivers and lakes were free of ice, and that meant the roads were open for the canoes. Guillaume had known all along what he would do when the ship finally went from his sight and the tie that bound him to Monsieur le Comte was severed: he would follow the river, too, but the other way. Into the unknown he would go as he made the life of a voyageur his. What did it matter that he had never been to the pays d'en haut? He knew what was required of a voyageur, and what he did not know he could soon learn.

"Adieu!" He raised his hand in farewell to the past and salute to the future; then he turned and walked rapidly to the small building that stood a short distance back from the wharf. His fingers made a *rat-a-tat-tat* on the door; his hand pushed it open, and he walked in.

The room was filled with wares—piles of cloth, cooking vessels, iron axes, chisels and spears, knives, guns, and boxes containing musket balls; there were many kegs, some holding gunpowder; others, high wine; there were bags of sugar and flour, trays holding beads, buttons, thimbles and trinkets. The smell of tobacco made the air rich. There was enough vermilion paint in dried blocks to cover a church. Guillaume stared. So much there was, it was hard to find his way among the bales and kegs and trays. Through and around them all he went to the far end of the room. There, by the one window, a man sat at a table, his gray head bent over the lists he was making, his hand moving occasionally to enter an item in a ledger beside him.

Guillaume waited until Bénédict Beaulieu, clerk-agent of La Compagnie Pelleterie, had finished one of his notations; then he made his presence known. "Bonjour, Monsieur."

Bénédict looked up at him. "Who are you and what do you want?"

Guillaume smiled. Dare the most or lose all, he told himself. Speaking more loudly than was called for, to give him confidence, he said: "Me? I am a voyageur! I would go to the pays d'en haut when the canoes go." He held his breath, hoping the agent would believe what he had yet to prove.

"They are going now," Bénédict replied as he reached under the ledger for a particular piece of paper.

Watching him, Guillaume let his breath out slowly, relieved that he had apparently persuaded the agent of his ability and his intent.

"Already we are loading at Lachine, and we need more men," Bénédict went on. "Never have there been so many wares to go north or so many furs to be brought back. The winter was good." He looked up from the paper and at the new recruit.

The young man standing by the table appeared to be

small in size, but that was no disadvantage. His slight, wiry body looked strong, and he was deep-chested. He did not have the stooped shoulders and bandy legs of a true voyageur, but that would come in time. His eyes were sharp, and that was an asset as much as his strong arms. His coppery skin and dark, silky hair told of his mixed parentage. Bénédict nodded. "What's your name?" he growled, as he dipped his quill into the inkpot and held it poised over the paper.

"I write my own name, s'il vous plaît."

Bénédict pushed the paper toward Guillaume. "Read the conditions, then sign."

Guillaume read the terms of the engagement that held him to three seasons at a pay of four hundred livres a season. By signing, he agreed not to desert or give aid to any rival company. Taking the quill, he dipped it again; then, in the fine French hand he had learned from Monsieur le Comte, he wrote *Guillaume Puissante.*

Bénédict studied it. "A voyageur who can write his own name! That's a new one. Where's your mother from?"

"She was a Chippewa, but she went back to her own people many years ago."

"And your father?"

Guillaume shrugged his shoulders, opened his hands wide, and smiled.

Bénédict nodded sympathetically. "Eh bien, he gave you his name; that's more than many of them do. You half-breeds are all the same, but you make the best canoemen. What can you do besides paddle?"

"I can sing."

"So!" Bénédict sat back in his chair and crossed his legs comfortably. "Chantez-moi."

Guillaume backed away from the table and leaned against a pile of blankets waiting to be baled. As a lover going through a garden would pick a rose for his beloved, he drew from memory the song that spoke as no other song to the heart of a voyageur, *En Roulant Ma Boule.*

He hummed through the tune once; then, in an easy, almost conversational way he began the story of the three white ducks who were swimming on a pond and of the prince who came riding by and with his silver gun shot one of the ducks. Melancholy began to tinge his tone when he sang of the diamonds that gleamed in the duck's eyes and of the blood that dripped from its wings, but gaiety returned as he sang of the three ladies who came across the field to gather the white duck's feathers and make them into a bed. Then laughter, sly but irrepressible, rippled through his singing as he hinted of the purpose to which the feather bed would be put and of what would sometime come from it, " 'Children big and children small.' "

Whenever he reached the chorus, he paused for a quick indrawing of breath; then the beat became more vigorous, as if he were calling to others to join in with him:

> " 'Roulite roulant
> Ma boule roulant.
> Roulite roulant
> Boule roulant,
> En roulant ma boule
> Qui roule,
> En roulant ma boule.' "

Bénédict, leaning far back in his chair with half-closed eyes, saw it all as he had seen it when he sang the song as a child with other children in the sunny courtyard of his home in France. He smiled as he recalled the first kiss he had ever given to a little girl. His feet began to tap to the tune of the game he had played long ago. He closed his eyes as the song went on, for he was a child no longer, but a young bourgeois in New France on his first trip into the pays d'en haut. The men had sung as they paddled in calm weather or gales, over smooth water or rough, in blazing heat or biting cold, at the start of a long day and at its dusky end, and the singing had given them endurance. It was not the words or even the tune, but something else that lifted their spirits and kept them soaring.

Bénédict opened one heavily lidded eye and watched the young man who was leaning against the pile of blankets. Because the words of the song had all been sung Guillaume hummed the tune by way of ending while his gaze roamed around the crowded warehouse. Bénédict took his time to open his eyes fully and then respond.

"Eh bien, bravo, mon voyageur. Your breath serves you well."

A smile, born of pride and pleasure, swept Guillaume's face. "In the tribe they used to call me Brother-of-the-Beaver because I could swim underwater for so long." He tapped his chest with the fingers of his right hand. "It is good, too, for singing."

"So!" Bénédict exclaimed, "you are a voyageur who can swim, too! Not all can do that."

"C'est trop fort! That is hard to believe."

Bénédict leaned forward and made a notation under the name on the paper. "Those who sing can always paddle; it is not so that those who paddle can always sing."

Guillaume smiled politely.

"How long have you been holding a paddle?"

Guillaume's shoulders went up expressively. "Can I say? In the tribe I was given one very small, and then ones that were bigger. All my life, m'sieu."

"All your sixteen years?"

The question required no answer.

"Eh bien, you know the conditions to which you have signed your name. You must also know that for your singing you will receive double, but on your return."

"C'est entendu. It is understood."

"You have your possibles?"

"No, Monsieur Bénédict, I—" Again he resorted to a gesture.

"Ça va!" Bénédict exclaimed good-humoredly. "You voyageurs are all the same. You wear so little that you wear it out and return almost in the state in which you were born. You gave your cap, I'll wager, to the first Indian maid who looked at you. But your sash, Guillaume Puissante, a voyageur never parts with his ceinture fléchée."

Guillaume put his hands on the table and looked earnestly at Bénédict Beaulieu. "Shall I tell you, m'sieu, what became of my sash? Shall I sing you my song about it?"

"Another time. The hour is late, and I have many lists still to make." He picked up the quill and waved Guillaume away with it. "On the bench near the door is a bundle wrapped in a capote. It will provide you with what you most need. Go now, and sing me your song some other day."

"And when do I leave, Monsieur Bénédict, for the pays d'en haut?"

"Tomorrow, from this office. The next day, or the day after, from Lachine. The canoes were brought there from winter storage a week ago and they have been in the water for repair, then loading. The first brigade has already left; you will be in the second. It leaves when loaded, and at dawn, always at dawn."

Guillaume bowed slightly, "Merci, m'sieu." He had accepted his work as a voyageur, its conditions and duration. At the door, he picked up the small bundle on the bench and tucked it under his arm.

Outside and on the wharf again, he did not look east up the river to where it led to the sea, but west to where it came out of the wilderness. Then, turning swiftly away from the river to the city growing toward the slopes of Mount Royal, he ran up the steep cobbled street to the château where Monsieur le Comte had so recently lived when commandant. Past the sentries, who knew him well, and in the rear entrance he went, then down the curving stone stairs to the kitchen to share his good fortune with the servants who were his friends.

"C'est moi," he announced, as he set his bundle down by the great fireplace. Impatient as he was to tell them his news, they had some for him that was even more urgent.

"Where have you been so long, Guillaume? The new commandant is giving a dinner tonight, and he wants you to sing for him."

"I have been at the wharf to watch *Le Cygne Chantant* sail away to France."

"But that was this morning!"

"When she sailed, yes; but it was long past noon when the white sails disappeared into the blue."

The cook came up to him with a cut from the roast that was slowly turning on the spit; with it was a generous piece of bread. "You must be hungry, Guillaume. Eat this, and you shall have more if you wish, for you have work to do."

"Yes, now that there is food, I am hungry and I shall eat."

While he ate they told him more of what was expected of him, not on this night only but for many nights. "There will be feasts and dancing and gaiety for weeks to come. That is always the way when a new commandant comes to the château. You will be called on to sing to them every night."

Guillaume shook his head, laughing. "Moi!" he said, as soon as he had finished eating, "I shall sing to them all night long—of France till their eyes swim with longing, of love till they melt like the wax in a candle with desire. I shall sing till they fall asleep over their wine cups; then no more shall I sing."

"No more? But he will ask you again; he will command."

"Ça ne fait rien. I am my own master now. I am a voyageur!"

Chapter Two

THAT NIGHT, WHEN the feast was nearly over and the call came for entertainment, Guillaume did what was expected of him. He went up to the dining hall, and while a fiddler scraped out a tune, Guillaume sang and danced before the people at the long table. Flinging his agile body about with a gay abandon, he stopped at times to lean across the table and drain a wineglass or to answer the beckoning finger of one of the guests; then bending his head close to the bearded lips, he would nod at the request for a particular song. Singing it zestfully, he relished the applause that came at the end as the guests beat with their spoons on their pewter plates or with bones that had been well cleaned.

Guillaume watched for the first sign of drooping lids, for the first head that leaned in rest against the carved back of a chair; then he signed to the fiddler to leave the room and the entertainment to him. Sitting down on the floor in front of the long table, Guillaume started to sing in a different manner a different type of song. He might have been a young mother crooning over a cradle, lulling her babe to sleep. Smiles curved over lips, eyes closed dreamily, fingers drummed in slow accompaniment on the table. Every man present who had come to New France for fame or fortune, honor or reprieve, was back in Old France where life was gentle and gracious, and love for the taking hung like apples on a laden tree. Guillaume sang ever more softly; then he hummed the melody only. He got to his feet and stood still; soon he moved slowly from the room, noiseless as a spring breeze.

Going down the stairs, he stopped by one of the narrow windows long enough to see that the night was beginning to gray; but the hour before dawn was always a long one. Entering the empty kitchen, he went toward the hearth where the stones were still warm from the fire that had burned there when the dinner was being cooked. A bowl of food had been left for him. He ate it hungrily, then took some bread and cleaned the bowl with it till it looked as if it had been washed. Curling up like a cat with a full belly in a warm nook, he gave himself to sleep.

But not for long. As soon as the first finger of light found its way through the high windows, Guillaume stirred. Uncurling himself from his ball of sleep and warmth, he crossed the room to the barrel of water that stood in a corner. Dipping some out into a bucket, he drank first, then washed the sleep from him.

The bundle wrapped in the capote was where he had left it the night before, and he unfolded it, discovering, as Monsieur Bénédict had told him, the garb he would need —breechcloth, deerskin leggings and moccasins, two blue shirts and a red cap, a large kerchief, and a sac-à-feu, a small beaded bag that was empty but for the strong smell of tobacco within it. Nothing was new. Most likely they had been the possibles of a voyageur who had not returned, but they were no worse than the jerkin and leggings he was wearing, and he was glad to exchange his clumsy boots for the flexibility of moccasins. Before donning them, he pressed them to his lips and breathed a prayer for the soul of the man who once had worn them. The shirt hung too loose without a sash to belt it, but the cap fitted well.

How would he have explained the loss of a sash, he asked himself, as he recalled his brave offer made to Monsieur Bénédict. No song he knew could have helped him, but the singing would. A story would have grown with the song, though not from his memory. Guillaume slapped his bare thighs at the thought. It was well that a song had not been asked for. He looked at his little pile of clothes on the hearth as a snake might look at his sloughed-off skin; no longer did they have any meaning for him. He took a piece of bread from the big loaf on the table and crossed the kitchen to the door that led outside.

The door had a way of groaning on its heavy hinges when it was opened wide, but Guillaume's slight body needed so little space that the door was not given a chance to protest. For a moment he stood still in the slice of golden sunlight that came into the kitchen, and looked at his familiar world. "Adieu," he said, more with his lips than with his voice; then he went out and closed the door behind him, knowing as he did so that he was closing it not on a single room but on most of the life that he could remember; knowing, too, that this door would not open again for him. Other doors might, but not this one. So it must be, for the château was no longer his world, though it had given him shelter for most of the years of his growing. Once before a door had closed behind him, a different kind of door; but he had been so young at the time that he remembered little about it.

Always, for a portion of each year, he had gone back to the tribe with his Indian mother, making their skills and their ways his. Then it had not seemed as if he had consciously learned anything, but as if things were awakened in him that were part of him. He swam because the water was there; he climbed because a tree invited him; he paddled because he found himself kneeling in a canoe with a paddle in his hands. It was different when Monsieur le Comte showed him how to read, then to write, and taught him all the songs he knew. Guillaume had had to make a conscious effort to learn; but once the new ways became his, they belonged to him as did the skills of woods and waters. Both ways of life belonged to him—one so natural, one that bespoke effort, yet to neither one did he seem to belong, and this had puzzled him. If he would question, he had no words then with which to shape a question, and no one who could have given him an answer.

One year, when the time of shortening days had come, the time when he and his mother always returned to the château, they walked through the forest together. She, who spoke rarely, was more silent than ever, and she moved slowly. Guillaume had hoped that, at the place where the forest yielded to cleared land and gave them their first glimpse of the city rising up against the sky, she would want to race toward it as he did. Winters were long and dark and cold in the forest; in the château there were warmth and light, certainty of food, and noisy, friendly people. When they came to the clearing, his mother had given him a thrust from behind, and Guillaume had run forward, laughing and eager. He would race her to the gates and she would be glad again.

Running the distance that he could shoot an arrow

from a bow, he suddenly realized that she was not running with him. He stopped and turned in his tracks, but she was nowhere to be seen, and where she had been was the green curtain of the forest: upstanding spruce, hemlock with low-sweeping branches, dark and silent. He had run back, calling her name, but at the fringe of trees he had stopped. In the soft earth at the edge of the clearing were his own small footprints. Beside the press of his mother's moccasined feet was the imprint of larger feet, those of the brave who had followed them so often during that summer. Guillaume backed away from the trees toward the cleared land, and as he did so the forest closed like a door upon a life that had been his, but never wholly.

He sat down on the earth, and everything within him seemed to melt. He could not see the forest, but on turning himself slowly around he could not see the city either. After a few moments he had stiffened his back and got to his feet. He rubbed his hands over his eyes, lifted his head, and stood at attention as he had seen soldiers do in the château courtyard when they received their orders. As an Indian, he could not cry; as a Frenchman, he could always sing.

He ran across the clearing, swift as a hare and singing like a bird. That night, when Monsieur le Comte had sent for him he could not explain why he was alone. He could say only that he was alone, and shrug his small thin shoulders as he had seen Frenchmen do when there were no words.

Monsieur le Comte had remained silent for a long moment, and the look on his face was the look of sorrow. When he spoke, his words were measured. "Ah, Guillaume, le seul péché c'est de trahir l'amour. The only sin is the betrayal of love." Then he started to sing. Lifting the boy up on his knees, he taught him yet another one of the songs that had been sung by troubadours in that faraway world of France.

Guillaume could not have said how old he was at that time, for years were marked more by events than by numbers. It was The Year the Snow Piled High or The Year of the First Communion or The Year of the Good Wine from France or The Year of the Long Sickness. But, numbered or named, they went on, and he grew through them. He learned to read and write, to sing and commit many long verses to memory. Before he knew what love was he sang about it; and knowing well only the cobbled streets and the wharves of Montréal, he sang of cities in France, of kings and queens, knights and ladies as if they were his familiars. The years that had stretched him in some ways and stunted him in others were all behind him now, and on them had closed a door as the forest door had closed.

The folded capote under one arm and the other swinging free, he ran down the street on his way to the office at the wharf.

An old woman, opening her door to let in the morning, called to him, "Where are you going, Guillaume?"

"To the pays d'en haut," he replied.

"Bonne chance," and she smiled, putting her fingers to her lips to blow him a kiss since he had not passed near enough to be given one.

He passed a woman sweeping her walk; from behind her full skirts a small girl was peeping. Guillaume bent down swiftly and gave the child a kiss; then he swung the mother's hand to his lips.

"Holà, Guillaume!" she exclaimed, "but it's not the Kissing Season."

"Non?" his shoulders went up so that they all but touched his ears. "The first day of the year or the first day of a venture, quelle différence?"

"Where are you bound?"

"Moi? Je suis voyageur."

"A voyageur without a sash?"

"But with a cap!" He spun around like a top and sang the refrain of *Youpe! Youpe! Sur la Rivière!*

> " 'Youpe! Youpe! sur la rivière,
> Vous ne m'entendez guère,
> Youpe! Youpe! sur la rivière,
> Vous ne m'entendez pas.' "

The woman went on with her sweeping in time with the song. The little girl came from behind the swaying skirts to clap her hands. Then the woman caught the spinning boy and held him to her.

"Guillaume, you are so young! A voyageur's life is a hard one, and not all come back in October who set out in May."

"So? And will all in Montréal who greet this fine morning greet a morning five months hence?"

"But you are so small, Guillaume!"

"They would not have given me a place in the canoe were I large. I thank le bon Dieu that I am as I am."

"When will you be back?"

"Dieu connaît!" Guillaume put his hand to his head to doff his red cap. He pressed one kiss, then another, on each of the woman's plump cheeks and was out of her embrace and on his way down the street before she could say more.

Singing as he walked, he moved his right arm as if it already held a paddle. He found it a useful position for throwing his arm about any chance girl he met as he bade them all a lighthearted farewell. By the time he reached the office of La Compagnie Pelleterie, he had a demiscore of stolen kisses to his account, and one that had been returned with such fervor that it had sent him reeling and momentarily deprived of the breath to sing.

Standing outside the office was a group of canoemen surrounded by their wives and children, half-breeds, all of them. Some of the men were more Indian than French; all were dark-skinned, with long black hair and drooping mustaches. Older than Guillaume Puissante, they were little different in stature, slight, wiry, well muscled. The stoop of their shoulders and the bandyness of their legs told of the years they had been carrying heavy packs and sitting in canoes. With flashing smiles, the men greeted the arrival of each new member of their group. Excitement was in the air, impatience in their movements. The close comfort of women and children had gone on long enough; open waters, dark forests, work, and the camaraderie of their own kind were what the men wanted now.

Guillaume stood in their midst, smiling into their faces as if they were all old friends, though not one had he ever seen before.

"You have no woman to bid you farewell?" one asked, as if commenting on a man with only one arm.

"Woman!" Guillaume threw back his head, and laughed. "There would not be room on this wharf if I brought my women. My farewells have all been said."

The voyageur's eyebrows went up. "You, so young!"

Another asked in a subdued tone. "How many?"

Guillaume opened his right hand and held its fingers up to the light; then he did the same with his left hand.

He could boast as well as the best and oldest of the voyageurs. As he surveyed his hands he started singing *Le Coeur de Ma Bien-aimée.*

It was a sentimental song, long known to voyageurs, and one of which they were particularly fond. The men formed a circle around Guillaume and sang with him. Because the song was about love, and love was something they would know only as they sang about it during the hard days in the wilderness, one man after another left the circle to have a last embrace with his own bien-aimée. When he returned, he sang more lustily than ever.

The women and children began to gather into their own small clusters, began to drift away, slowly, wistfully, with many a backward glance. Their men were theirs no longer, nor would they be until winter brought the long canoes back again. Some moved off with brisk determination; others with relief, as if at last something could be done about the house now that a man and his lovemaking would be out of it for five months; a few, and among them those already large with the future, lingered, hoping for one more kiss, one more word.

Drawn by the sound of the singing, Bénédict Beaulieu looked up from his work and went to stand in the doorway of his office. It was many years since he had been in a canoe, but he remembered that particular song well and, joining in with the men as they sang, he felt himself young again. The light of the May morning was sharp and fresh; beyond the wharf the river rippled gaily. Bénédict was caught up in the rhythm of the song. His feet began tapping; his hand that for years had held nothing weightier than a quill pen raised itself as if holding a paddle, and moved down, then up again. He longed to be one of them, to be again slight of body, keen of eye, and to be setting out on the journey to the pays d'en haut. There was a tug at his heart for the way of life and the work to which he assigned men every season and from which he paid those that returned.

He watched and sang, inwardly pleased that his voyageurs could go through the motions of their work even before the time to take up their work had come. It was a good omen. Perhaps they would reach Grand Portage with fine weather and against few odds; perhaps they would all return. The song ended with a shout as it should, as its words climbed to the Gates of Paradise and made their demand of St. Peter for the heart of the well-beloved.

The crowd of men began to break apart as the one who had led the singing went toward the office.

Bénédict was not surprised to see that it was Guillaume Puissante.

"Bonjour, Monsieur Bénédict."

"You sing so well, Guillaume, that men would paddle even without a canoe."

"So?" Guillaume looked surprised. "I told you, m'sieu, that I sang. Are there other ways of singing? I know only one."

Turning in from the doorway and going toward his table, Monsieur Bénédict said, "I hope you paddle as well."

"Why not?"

"Eh bien"—Bénédict shuffled among the papers on his desk—"you have come to ask about the place I have assigned you."

"I have come to ask you for a sash, m'sieu. Voilà!" Guillaume held out his blue shirt to show how long and full it was. "I am no voyageur without a sash."

"You who sing about love, do you not know that your sash must be given you by a woman? Only then are you sure to return. My little granddaughter has made you a sash. I knew there was none in that bundle, and you said you had lost yours. Look at you; that shirt flaps like the wings of a gull. Tina!" he called; then he repeated the name.

From a room back of the office a voice could be heard, "Je viens, pépé."

A girl appeared holding a sash in her hands. She went up to Guillaume and offered it to him. "Votre ceinture fléchée."

With a graceful gesture and a murmur of thanks, he took it from her, held it up for full view, then put it around his waist and tied it, lightly at first and until his shirt was well caught in it; then he tightened it gradually. "It is like the rainbow."

"It is a good piece of woven wool from France," Bénédict explained, "and Tina has sewed the seams well."

Guillaume smiled appreciatively at the girl who waited for his approval. She stood before him sturdy and straight, with apple-plump cheeks, sparkling blue eyes, and straw-colored braids. He bent down and kissed her. "Merci, ma petite," he said.

"À votre service," Tina replied; then, laughing merrily, she ran back to the room that was part of the small dwelling where she kept house for her grandfather.

"C'est beau," Guillaume said, patting his sash and letting his fingers run down the length of the fringe that reached to his knees.

"And it serves, how the sash serves!" Bénédict nodded. "You live in Montréal, Guillaume; it is your home?"

Guillaume gestured widely with his arms. "The world

is now my home, m'sieu. Until yesterday I was a servant at the château, but since le commandant returned to France I am my own master."

Bénédict studied the young face shrewdly, watched the fingers as they went back to playing with the sash. "When you return, Guillaume, you may call this your home. There is much work to do, getting the furs ready for shipment in the spring, making the bills of lading. Tina can keep house for us both."

"Monsieur—"

Bénédict waved away the words. "When a man goes to the pays d'en haut, Guillaume, he must know that he has a place of return."

"Merci" was too small a word. Guillaume dropped to one knee and pressed Monsieur Bénédict's hand to his lips.

"Ça va," Bénédict growled; then he devoted his attention to a sheet of paper on the table before him. "With the brigade that leaves tomorrow, I have a place for you. Now, let me see what place it is."

While Bénédict shuffled among his papers, Guillaume prayed fervently, not only to le bon Dieu as most people did, or to la Sainte Vierge, but to an army of saints named and unnamed, as well as the Rain God, the Sun God, and the One who kept the winds in a bag and who could be fierce as well as friendly. It had always seemed to Guillaume that the greater the area of intercession, the more apt the prayer was to be answered.

"Let it be a place in the middle, in the very middle of the canoe, for this first journey. Let it be—oh, let it be—for only le bon Dieu knows all that I do not know."

Bénédict talked to himself as he read over the names on the sheet before him. "I have need for a bowman on my

Number Two canoe, and for a steersman on my Number
Six. . . ."

Guillaume began his silent intercession all over again,
adding any saint or god he might have left out who could
have been offended by the omission. "Not a bowman, O
Holy Ones," he breathed inwardly. "Not a steersman, I beg
you." Those were the two positions that he knew bore the
full responsibility for the canoe. A submerged rock not
seen by the bowman, a false turn made by the steersman,
and all could be in jeopardy.

"And you've done this before," Bénédict said without
looking up.

Guillaume's lips felt dry. "Bien sûr, of course." The
words, barely whispered, did not mislead the man who
had engaged him.

Then Guillaume thought of one last recourse, the
Guardian Angel of Monsieur Bénédict Beaulieu, the one
who, though invisible, was in the room with them and had
been all along. "In the middle, please, Saint Seigneur, in
the very middle of the canoe. With all my heart I promise
I will watch so well that at another time I may sit in
another place, but this first time let it be in the middle, s'il
vous plaît."

Bénédict went on mumbling to himself until he had
made his decision. With the chart of the Number Three
canoe before him, he pointed to a particular place. "Left
side, au milieu, from Lachine to Grand Portage. Singing
goes best from the center of the canoe."

The noise made by the unrolling of a map drowned the
sound of Guillaume's long-held breath as it escaped him.

The map covered most of the table. On it Bénédict

pointed to the route, moving the feather tip of his quill over lakes and along rivers. In the far right corner was Montréal; in the opposite corner was their immediate destination, Grand Portage. Across the distance flowed a dark, irregular line — the Ottawa River widening into Lake Nipissing, narrowing again into the French River, and narrowing alarmingly at the Sault-Sainte-Marie, then opening out on to the Great Lake whose waters they skirted to bring them to Grand Portage. As the quill indicated the course, Bénédict accounted for the miles. "Two thousand, and with good weather you will be at Grand Portage by the first of July."

"And is that the end of our journey?"

"La fin?" Bénédict made a rumbling noise in his throat. "Mais non, ce n'est que le commencement."

Guillaume realized his mistake and caught it quickly. "Pardon, m'sieu, of course it is the beginning of the second part." The map went no farther than Grand Portage. Where the next road lay he would discover only after the first road had been covered.

"You are lucky, Guillaume. The brigade that sets out tomorrow is composed of new canoes, built last winter at Three Rivers and only recently brought down to Lachine. They are ten of my finest, part of the squadron of thirty canoes."

"Dieu merci."

Bénédict reached into his pocket and brought out a new clay pipe that he handed to Guillaume. "Fill your sac-à-feu with some tobacco from my can; tuck your pipe in sash. Now you are a voyageur. Go, and let your hair grow long to protect your neck from the insects."

Guillaume's thanks were well matched with his exhilaration. He slapped his bare thighs and laughed gaily. "Au revoir, Monsieur Bénédict."

"Yes, until we meet again."

Guillaume filled the beaded pouch and attached it to his sash; beside it he thrust the clay pipe; then he left the office to join the men on the wharf. Some had already started down the road that followed the river to the village of Lachine; others were leaving. Each man carried on his back one of the ninety-pound pièces of wares that were to go in the canoes; the remaining pièces were piled in an ox-cart. Some of the people who had come to see the men off walked along beside them for awhile; others returned to the city. Waving their caps, the voyageurs shouted goodbyes; looking back, they took a last glimpse of church spires with gilded crosses, rooftops, and windows shining in the sunlight, smoke curling from chimneys, people going about their business. Then, looking ahead, they let their eyes rest on the river, the distant forests, the rich world of the fur trade.

Lachine was the point from which adventurers and traders had gone into the wilderness since the time when Jacques Cartier had sought a route to China. It was La Salle's men, two hundred years later, who had given the place its name in ridicule.

The voyageurs marched gaily, each one bent slightly into the wind under the weight of his pièce; each one boasting that he could easily have carried another if someone had been there to hoist it onto his shoulders. The pièces contained the goods that would be exchanged with the Indians for furs, and they contained provisions for the journey. Well wrapped as they were, the men rarely knew what they carried. Only the keg of high wine proclaimed itself as it sloshed, and the man who bore it on his back made a play of dropping it. His comrades could laugh, for they knew well that only an old sure-footer was ever given this cargo to carry. Had he dropped and cracked it, a season's work without pay might have been the cost to him.

The dock at Lachine was well beyond the foaming rapids, and havened from the swift flowing of the river. There, ten canots de maître were tied. They were slender and high-prowed, each one some thirty-five to forty feet in length and weighing some three hundred pounds. Fourteen men were required to handle one of the canoes. Though they looked fragile and light, when loaded, each canoe could sustain a weight of five tons. Some, already loaded, rested low in the water; others, yet to be loaded, rode high. All through the morning the loading went on. Long poles were laid in the bottoms of the canoes, and on these were placed sixty pièces to a canoe, which constituted the cargo; the provisions included six hundredweight of biscuits, two hundredweight of lard, and three bushels of peas, as well as a keg of high wine. Two large cloths were carried to cover both cargo and provisions, as well as a sail, an ax, a towline, a kettle for cooking, and various items for repair—strips of birchbark, spruce gum, and watap.

As the loading went on, the men took their orders from old François Gilbert, who studied, fitted, placed, and arranged everything as it should be for safety and convenience in the ten canoes that made up the brigade. Too old now to paddle, François knew to an ounce and an inch the capacity of a canoe and where and how its load should be disposed. Each pièce was given its own distinguishing mark in vermilion paint so that, when the canoe was unloaded at a portage or a night's camp, it could be reloaded exactly as it had been at the dock at Lachine. By the time any one of the canoes was loaded and ready to embark, François could have told with his eyes closed where each pièce rested and where the remaining freight had been stored. He knew where each voyageur would sit, the thwart assigned to him with the space beneath it available for his small bundle of possibles. By the time the sun had begun to set, all the canoes were loaded. Gunnels were within six inches of the water. When the men took their places, the gunnels would be scarcely an inch above the water.

"À demain. At the sun's rising." François dismissed with a gesture the men who had been working under his orders all during the day.

Cheerful and shouting, the men went off to the small stone building that stood a few steps away from the dock. There, they knew, would be food and warmth for them, a cask of wine, and a dry place to sleep. It would be the last such night they would have for many months.

François remained standing, looking at the high prows as they caught the sun's last rays; then he sat down on one of the pièces that awaited another brigade, another day's loading. He took his pipe from his sash, his sac-à-feu from beside it, and started to make preparations for a smoke.

Guillaume approached him. "You do not come with us for food, Monsieur François?"

"Not I. All night I stay with my canoes. I will not see them again until the leaves on the trees are as red as those high prows." He stuffed the bowl of his pipe with tobacco, lit it with his fire steel, and puffed until smoke curled around his mustache.

"I stay with you." For the third time that day Guillaume tied his sash tighter to stave off the hunger that was within him.

"Bien. You are not hungry?"

"I eat when there is food."

"Très bien. You speak like a voyageur. But I do not remember seeing you set out last season?"

"No? You will not forget me another year." Guillaume sat down beside François, drew his pipe out from its place in his sash, and held it in his hands.

François put his fingers into his own beaded pouch and pinched out some tobacco. "The first puff is for luck," he said as he took Guillaume's pipe from him and stuffed tobacco into its bowl. "The second is for memory."

"Merci, m'sieu."

As darkness settled down, the water that had been rippling so merrily all day stilled; with the darkness came silence. It seemed to come out of the vastness into which the high prows were facing and wrap itself around the two who sat on the dock puffing peacefully at their pipes. The sounds of laughter and revelry that came from the building close by increased, then diminished gradually. Before all sound had ceased, one of the men came from the stone house with a wooden trencher of food and a small flask of wine.

"It is enough for us both," François said.

Guillaume loosened his sash and put away his pipe.

As they ate and quaffed together, François spoke reminiscently of the pays d'en haut. Guillaume felt, as he listened, that this was not being done for his benefit but that François would have talked as he did had no one been here. He would have spoken to the night, to the canoes with their waiting loads, to the unknown that lay ahead for the voyageurs. He was like a lover telling of his beloved, but the words were those of a man fiercely proud of his calling and glorying in it with a joy undimmed by time or age.

He spoke of the smooth and shining waters over which the canoes would race; of the turbulent waters in which they would fight their ways when only the combined skill and strength of every voyageur could keep a canoe on its course. "Sing then, mon ami, as you have never sung before but as you will many times again. Sing, and the more savage the wind, the sweeter be your song."

He spoke of rapids that defied passage, where the canoes would have to be unloaded and both contents and canoe portaged to a place where the water ran smooth again; of other rapids over which the loaded canoe could be cordelled as the men with lines attached towed it as they walked along the shore; and he spoke of rapids that could be run. "For the man who steers remembers the rocks and can go between them, and the man in the bow is always swift to see and act. When you are running rapids, mon ami, pray to all the saints in heaven, but do what the steersman commands."

Guillaume shivered.

"You are cold? Unfold your capote; that is what it is for."

"Mais oui!" Guillaume laughed with relief.

François smiled tenderly at the boy, so tired and ready for sleep yet so eager to take in all that was being told him. François sensed that, for all his brave ways, the new recruit was facing the pays d'en haut for the first time, and the old man yearned to make the way safer from the experience he had gained during his long years as a voyageur.

"Danger speaks in a loud voice where water boils over

rocks and swirls around them, but there are places where danger speaks in no voice at all," François warned. "There are many places where the water may look smooth, and beneath lie rocks that could tear the bottom from a canoe or pierce a small hole that in time would be as bad. The steersman remembers these places. In his memory he carries a chart. He who has grazed a canoe once will not do so again, for a voyageur would rather die than do his work carelessly," he paused.

Guillaume's eyebrows went up as if in query; then he nodded in agreement.

"At many points along the way you will see crosses on the shore," François said. "Look well to them and mark them in your memory, for where men have died men may die again. Danger stalks a canoe like a wolf its prey; laugh at the danger but respect the cause."

"When the danger is great I shall sing."

"Yes, sing, and see that all in the canoe do likewise so no one will have breath for fear. Ah, mon ami, I am an old man now. For more than twenty seasons I have gone to the pays d'en haut, but I can do so no more. My joints are stiff and my muscles ache, but I have lived as a man! Voilà, better it is to die having lived than to be a beggar of life."

François reached for the flask. Seeing it still held wine, he tipped it first to his lips, and drank, then offered it to Guillaume. François looked dreamily into the night, at the stars in the sky and at those reflected in the river, and he thought of the promise such clarity held out for the next day. He was silent for a long time. Without talk between them there seemed to be no sound anywhere at all, but for the slight lap of the water against the waiting canoes; then he began to speak again.

"It is not all water and weather, mon ami. Sometimes those who live in the forest can give trouble. Safe in their own pursuits, they are harmless most of the time, but come between a she-bear and her cubs and she'll slash your cheek so that a woman will not look at you again. Wound a wolverine rather than kill it clean, and a new cross may be placed at a campsite. And, mon ami, an Indian does not always think like a Frenchman; I ask you to remember that."

Guillaume nodded soberly.

"There is something that a man cannot see with his eyes or combat with his arms, but he can hear it with his ears, and when he does he will ask, 'Is this my own ghost calling to me or is this the ghost of a canoe lost many years ago and have its men come back to warn or to lure?' This is the sound heard when a canoe passes through a narrows with high rock walls on either side and the men who have been singing cease and paddle silently but the singing goes on. Many a voyageur's heart will curdle with fear, and for the price of his soul he would turn back, but he cannot. You will fear then, mon ami, unless you know what it is." He paused, the long pause that might require no answer but to which Guillaume knew answer must be made.

"I have not feared, Monsieur François, when I have heard my own voice calling back to me from the walls of the château. I shall not fear when it calls to me in the pays d'en haut."

A slow smile, as proud as it was tender, crept over François's face. "You know, then, and you are safe. But Echo has led many a voyageur to his death."

The hours were moving on; and Guillaume, with hunger and thirst long satisfied, felt heavy with sleep. He wrapped his capote around him and prepared to curl up into a comfortable ball.

François, watching him, said, "You have no knife, mon ami, and that is not good, for a knife serves as does pipe, paddle, and sash."

"I have no knife, m'sieu."

François put his hand on his sash and unloosed his own knife. The blade, kept very sharp, was protected by the fur sheath in which it was housed; the handle was worn smooth from use. "À votre sûreté," François said as he presented the knife to Guillaume.

"Mais, monsieur—"

"Attach it to your sash, and then around your middle you will have all that a voyageur needs for his safety and comfort."

Guillaume did so, murmuring his thanks not once but a half-dozen times. Sleep had now quite gone from him, so he turned to look up at his friend. The bearded lips were parted as if to speak.

"There is yet another test, mon ami—"

Had François continued speaking, Guillaume might have been lulled again by the voice, and slipped into sleep. It was the pause that alerted him. "And what may that be, Monsieur François?"

"Ah—" Long drawn and honey sweet with memory was the sound made by the older man as he drew in his breath.

Guillaume uncurled himself enough to prop his head on his hands and let his eyes rest fully on François Gilbert. The glow from the pipe bowl illuminated the man's face. In it were wonder, bliss, joy, all fed by memory. Guillaume knew well what the pause meant. He had seen that expression more than once in Monsieur le Comte's face. "C'est l'amour," he said reverently.

François nodded and puffed more rapidly, so that his face shone like a statue in a church when an array of candles had been lit in front of it.

"Moi!" Guillaume exclaimed, "I keep my heart to myself." Then he unpropped his head, wrapped his arms around him to conserve his warmth, let the capote fall over him like a blanket, and gave himself to sleep. This time neither words nor pause could wake him.

"So! That is what you think now." François said as he settled himself comfortably against some pièces to watch the night retreat before the morning. As he did so, all his past life seemed linked to the moment. "And what better life can there be than to work hard, to sing and to love when one is young, and when one is old to have something worth reliving in memory. Je m'en souviens! I remember. Blest by le bon Dieu and his saints is the man who can say those words with a smile on his lips!"

Dawn came, and mist covered the river, veiling the past and the future.

"Venez! Venez!" François's command to come rang out crisply. He had a stack of paddles beside him, ready to give them to the voyageurs. There were short ones for the men in the center of the canoes, longer and wider ones for the steersmen, and for the bowmen the widest and strongest of all the paddles. The blades were red, and they had all been newly painted. By the time the canoes returned, only the tips of some of the paddles would still be vermilion; others would have been worn down to the wood and be the color of the cedar from which they were made.

Guillaume unrolled himself from sleep, bundled up his

belongings, and joined the men who came tumbling from the stone house where they had spent the night. Together, they went to a shallow place by the river where they could wash and refresh themselves. Shaking the water from their long hair, they donned their red caps, tied their sashes tight, and snatched some morsels of food from a vendor who had come out from Montréal. Every move was made quickly, punctuated only by laughter and brave words. Nothing mattered now but to receive their paddles, fall into line by one of the waiting canoes in their assigned places, and be ready to leap in when the word was given.

Guillaume, sharp of eye and eager for departure, watched what the voyageurs were doing, and did likewise.

François stood by the Number One canoe and called out the names of those who would man it. Veteran voyageurs all, each one stepped over the gunnel lightly, took his place, set his small bundle of possibles under his seat, then sat with paddle poised, bright vermilion tip just touching the water. The position was one that would not be changed until the first pipe was called or the first portage reached. The steersman got in and stood in position; last of all the bowman took his place near the curved prow. Ready: they waited for the word to go forward.

The Number Two canoe was loaded; then François stood beside the Number Three and called out the names: "Jean! Michel! Guillaume! Prosper! Pierre! Joseph! Hyacinth! Maurice! Hypolite! Baptiste! Nicolet! Paul! Martin! Henri! Prenez vos places!"

Swiftly, and so lightly that the canoe scarcely trembled at the action, they took their places and sat with paddles ready to cut the water. The added weight caused the craft to sink so that the gunnels were just above the surface.

François studied the clearance before moving on to the Number Four canoe. He knew about that inch and had planned for it. As they waited for the other canoes to load, the men who shared thwarts exchanged words with each other. Some were long familiar; others met for the first time.

Prosper put his left hand on Guillaume's knee; Guillaume covered it with his own left.

"We are well met, mon ami," Prosper said; then he peered piercingly into the face of the young man who sat so close to him.

Guillaume was aware of the dark eyes looking at him as they had long looked at the water over which he paddled to discern its depth or danger. Guillaume knew that he could hide nothing from those eyes. There was kindness in the lean brown face, in the lips curving under their silky mustache. Guillaume felt that he could trust Prosper.

"Listen well," the older voyageur warned, "and follow. Do not attempt to lead. That is for Martin who steers or Henri who bows; it is never for us au milieu."

Guillaume, relieved that Prosper understood, bowed his head slightly, "Je vous remercie."

Prosper laughed, withdrawing his left hand to give a light tap on Guillaume's shoulder. "De rien. We are friends, Guillaume."

Guillaume touched his hand to his cap in salute to their relationship.

By the time the tenth canoe was ready to leave, the priest could be seen coming toward them. The distance from the small chapel in Lachine was short, and he walked rapidly, the long skirts of his cassock flapping in the breeze of his movement. Standing near the canoes, he repeated prayers that no one could understand but in which each had perfect faith; then, lifting a crucifix high above his head, the priest blessed them all in good French words. Red-capped heads bowed, and left hands made the sign of the cross from brow to breast, from shoulder to shoulder; for nothing, not even for the priest himself, would right hands leave the paddles. A murmur of sound rose from the men as they followed the priest in prayer, "Notre Père, qui êtes aux cieux—"

"Le bon Dieu protect you, la Sainte Vierge look down on you, and may all the holy angels be with you and bring you safely back. Adieu, mes voyageurs!"

"Ainsi soit-il!" The sound of a hundred and forty voices, subdued no longer, but gay and audacious, swelled the air. Heads were raised; bodies leaned forward; paddle tips kissed the water.

"Allez-y!" François shouted, and the first canoe shot forward. "Allez-y et bon voyage!"

A minute later he gave the command to the second canoe, spacing them so there would be no crowding until they were well on their way in the Grand River.

From the height of Mount Royal a cannon boomed and flags waved in the bright morning light; but no man looked up or back or around. Each voyageur's eyes were on the water that his paddle would cut into; each man worked as if it were his paddle alone that propelled the whole canoe, while keeping time with the pace set by the bow-man. With wind and water in their favor they would do a stroke a second, and before an hour had passed some six miles of the river would be behind them.

"Chantez!" came the command from the steersman. Guillaume gave the pitch, clear and strong; then he began with the chorus of *En Roulant Ma Boule.* The voyageurs joined in immediately, singing as they paddled. Once the song had been started, it was Guillaume who sang the verses, and the men joined in when he came to:

> " 'Roulite roulant
> Ma boule roulant.
> Roulite roulant
> Boule roulant,
> En roulant ma boule
> Qui roule,
> En roulant ma boule.' "

After that he led them in *V'là l'Bon Vent!* The words of the many verses were the same, but the tune was different, as was the chorus:

> " 'V'là l'bon vent, v'là l'joli vent,
> V'là l'bon vent!
> M'ami' m'appelle.
> V'là l'bon vent, v'là l'joli vent,
> V'là l'bon vent!
> M'ami m'attend.' "

François watched the brigade as it sped down the river, aided by a light wind. Paddles flashed; loads rode well. His eyes were as pleased at the sight as were his ears with the sound of singing that drifted back to him. Behind him the sun had only just got itself above the distant hills, and its light was making a broad path of gold, almost as wide as the river itself, and in its path the canoes were traveling.

"Bien!" he exclaimed many times as he kept his eyes on them until the turn in the river took them from his sight. Tomorrow another brigade would leave; today there was loading to be done. Voyageurs would soon be arriving. But before work commenced again, he had a time-honored duty to discharge. Turning away from the dock, he followed in the wake of the priest up the street to the chapel.

François Gilbert moved slowly, conscious now of his years and his infirmities, but deep within him was an ache that had nothing to do with time or rheumatism. His good left arm would he gladly have given if he could have gone with the canoes, but that was not to be nor would it ever be for him again. He was an old man now, of small use but to see that the canoes were well loaded and to send them on their way.

"Ah, but someone must give orders," he sighed as he settled on a bench in the chapel and waited for the priest to begin the mass. A few villagers came in, a few voyageurs, crossing themselves and whispering brief prayers as they took their places. During the time when the canoes left for the pays d'en haut, masses were always said in the villages that bordered the river and in those from which voyageurs had come. François would pray for the safety of the canoes and their cargoes, as well as for the voyageurs who manned them; such was his duty, but le bon Dieu would understand if he offered a special prayer for one young voyageur.

"So young, Notre Père," he confided, with the intimacy always felt in the chapel, "that he has not even a mustache, and scarcely the beginning of one."

Chapter Three

ONCE ONLY DURING the first hour and during the whole first part of their journey did the canoes pause all together, though keeping careful distance from each other as they did so. At the shrine of Ste. Anne that had been erected many years ago when the first voyageurs went to the pays d'en haut, the ten canoes halted. Ste. Anne was the patron saint of the voyageurs, and no man would think of going into the perilous work before him without the blessing of her protection. Paddles were raised above their heads in salute, and red caps bowed while the canoes rocked gently from the last thrust that had been given and in the movement of the current. Each man made his supplication in the manner of the voyageur, praying for the one who sat beside him rather than for himself. The steersman in each canoe murmured a "Notre Père" in which the men joined, the whispering sound of their voices so different from the zestful sound of their singing.

The first canoe dipped its paddles and moved into the current; the second followed; the third; and all the rest in the brigade. They might see each other in the distance; they might catch the lilt of each other's songs; but they would not meet again until they were in the great lake ready for the advance to Grand Portage. They would not meet unless disaster overtook a canoe and help was needed; but that was not a likely event. They had asked Ste. Anne for her protection, and the knowledge that they were in her care gave each voyageur a confidence that complemented his courage.

"Now we are on our way," Prosper said to Guillaume, smacking his lips, for the taste of the future was good.

"C'est bien," Guillaume replied. There were a dozen questions he wanted to ask, but not one would ever find its way to his lips. He would watch, and his eyes would tell him, what other men did he could do. He breathed a private prayer of thanksgiving to any saint who might take the time to hear it that he had been placed in the middle of the canoe and that it was Prosper who shared the thwart with him.

"Do you know *Le Bâtiment Merveilleux?*"

"Mais oui!" Guillaume laughed at the thought that a song sung in so many districts over so many years should not be his.

Giving the pitch to get the attention of the other men, he began singing the story of the wonderful boat that had been built by the people of Boucherville. Its hull was made of an old tin box, and three stalks of mugwort were used for its masts. The rudder was the tail of an old white horse, and the sails were made from coarse fustian shirts. The captain was an old white-frontaled bull, and the cook was a cow aged thirty-three. The crew were springtide lambs that gamboled fore and aft—

> " 'And everyone aboard that ship
> Was quite definitely daft.' "

The voyageurs took to laughing so uproariously at the words that they joined in the chorus with even more vigor than usual:

" 'Gailonlà, brunette,
Gailonlà, gaîment!' "

When the known words came to an end, Guillaume went on with words of his own making; much to the delight of the voyageurs, who never wanted a good song to end unless it could be replaced by a better.

Singing lustily, paddling in unison, the canoe sped past an occasional clearing in the forest. Where a small river emptied into the great one, there was a settlement consisting of two or three houses, a cross-topped church, a mill with its wheel turning slowly. There were green fields where the land had been cleared for grazing, and brown fields where plowing was being done; but the clearings were small. A family raised only what it needed, and the fertile land gave generously. Behind the clearings, and often separating them from each other, was the forest with its riches of game and timber, and always there was the river with its fish: there was more than enough to eat, and every man had the same as his neighbor. Born to liberty and an equality unknown in Old France, the habitants were able to keep a comfortable balance between what they might want and what they needed to live well.

"They eat too much," Nicolet observed.

"Tant pis, we do not starve," Hyacinth, the cook, reminded him.

"Every man to his own," Pierre said, accenting his words with the thrust of his paddle.

A man stopped his work in a field to wave to the

voyageurs as they went by; then he watched them until they had gone from his sight. A woman, spinning in a doorway, caught the burden of the song they were singing, and sang it as she turned her wheel and fastened the fine wool around her distaff. A child, driving a flock of geese, lifted both hands to her lips and tossed kisses to the voyageurs; even the geese rose tall from their webbed feet and flapped their great ungainly wings in the direction of the canoe.

"Arrêtez et allumez," Martin, the steersman, called.

The respite was welcome. The men stopped paddling, laid their paddles carefully inside the canoe, and took from their sashes their pipes and tobacco pouches. After they had puffed quietly for a few minutes, they began to exchange comments about the settlement they had passed. Not one of them would have given his place in a canoe for a habitant's house, stock, and land.

"When I am old," Prosper said, "perhaps I would like the life, but not now, not now." He lifted his head and looked before him, away from the greening fields along the shore to the river threading its way into the wilderness.

After ten minutes or so Martin gave the call to go forward again. "Allons-y!" Pipes were put away, paddles were taken up, and the canoe resumed its course. The miles covered in a day's march could be fairly well measured by the number of pipes, for Martin called for one every four to six miles. Tobacco was used sparingly, and every deep-drawn breath was savored.

As they approached the landing for the first portage, Guillaume noticed that a cross made from a broken paddle had been placed there. Every voyageur pulled off his red cap, bowed his head, and uttered a prayer for the lost comrade, whether he had been known to them or not.

After saying his prayer, Prosper muttered: "But he was a fool, though may le bon Dieu bless his soul. A voyageur does not permit his paddle to become broken—" He said more, but his words were lost in the roar of the rapids that lay beyond the smooth water at the landing.

As with all their moves, it was speed and agility that counted. Before the prow of the canoe touched the shore, Martin leaped out and held the stern so the canoe would not graze its bottom on sand or stone; his move was followed by that of Henri who steadied the prow. Then, so swiftly that the movement seemed like that of one man rather than twelve, the voyageurs stepped over the gunnels and into the water to lift the canoe toward shore. Pièces and cargo were removed and laid on dry ground; the canoe was turned over; two men placed themselves at each end and raised it as two others placed themselves in the middle to take the rest of its weight on their shoulders, then they started off with it over the portage path to the smooth water beyond the rapids. The remaining men shouldered pièces and cargo and made as many trips as were necessary to get everything to the place where reloading and embarkation could be made. No words passed among them, for they would have been wasted in the din. The procedure was a familiar one, and Guillaume, by watching and following, soon made it his. As the distance covered on the water was measured by pipes, that on the land was measured by poses. Every third of a mile or so, a man set his load down and rested. Some portages were so short that no pose was required; others took anywhere from three to thirty.

The canoe was soon loaded, and the men sat in their places again, the final thrust off being given by Martin before he leaped over the gunnel to stand in the stern with his long paddle. Before moving into new water, the voyageurs pulled off their red caps, held them in their hands while making the sign of the cross, and listened as Martin repeated a prayer. With the last syllable of the "Ainsi soit-il," the caps were on their heads and the paddles taken up.

"Ah," Prosper chuckled, "how white must be our souls, for we say more prayers on a voyage than all the rest of the year in church!"

Paddles cut the water, and the canoe was on its way again. When they sang, they all sang together; when they were silent, they were all silent together. A canoe was no place for talk, but talk would have its place and time when they made camp for the night. Except for pipes and poses, their first day into the pays d'en haut had seen close to twelve hours of paddling. Some days would see fifteen hours, and a few eighteen hours; but they had been going against the current in the river, and it was their first day. Martin was pleased with the distance covered and the way the men had worked together; he was also pleased that before night's long shadow fell they had reached a good place to stop. It was where a small meadow sloped from the woods to the water and it gave room for the men to engage in their games while there was still light. The earth would provide as soft a bed as a voyageur could expect.

The canoe was unloaded, beached, upturned. The pièces were covered with large cloths made of canvas. Hyacinth, the cook, immediately began to prepare the meal for which the men would soon be ready. They had had nothing to eat since morning, and sashes had been tightened many times against the gnawing of hunger. Wood was gathered, a fire made, and the big kettle swung over it. Water was soon boiling in the kettle, and into it went hulled corn and lard with a seasoning of salt; a quart was allowed for each man, and by the time each had received his share the kettle would be empty.

While the meal was cooking, Martin and Henri went carefully over the seams of the canoe, its bottom and sides. They inspected every inch of it for the slightest graze or the least dent that could result in a leak the next day. The small kettle that held pitch had been placed near the fire, and from it they would use what was needed to seal a seam or repair a tear. The men amused themselves in the meadow, matching their skills and their strengths in games and, as they said, dusting each other's clothes in wrestling bouts. Once the call came from Hyacinth that the food was ready, they raced to the kettle by the fire and took what was given them. They ate quickly, as they did everything, so they could get to the best time of the day for a voyageur, the time when he stretched out at ease by the fire, smoked his pipe, and joined in the telling of stories. No matter how tall the story, there was always one taller, for no voyageur had ever known wind or water that could get the better of him; no voyageur had ever carried a load so heavy that it could not have been heavier; and no voyageur had ever been on a portage that was too long for him.

"La ronde! La ronde!" Pierre shouted, and the men with their fill of rest and talk behind them sprang up and into movement. Circling the fire, they sang and danced with a gaiety and freedom that defied the long day of work behind them and the short night of sleep before them. But the dance was soon over. First one man, then another, stumbled off into the dark to find his capote, wrap himself in it, and lie down to sleep. Only then was Guillaume mindful of his weary body, but so quickly did drowsiness merge into sleep that he felt the cold ground against his bare buttocks no more than he heard the lapping of the water on the shore.

"Alerte, lève, lève, nos gens!" Hyacinth called.

Darkness still held, but the first hint of light had come in the east, and that meant only one thing to the voyageurs.

Like soldiers responding to reveille, they rolled out of sleep, folded their capotes, made their brief preparations for the day, ate a bellyful of the corn and pork that must stand by them till they made camp again, then helped in the loading of the canoe. All was done in less than a quarter of an hour. They moved swiftly about the known tasks, but once in the canoe with paddles touching the water they paused for the prayer said before anything new, be it a day, or a lake.

"Allons-y!" Martin's cry cut the silence, and they were off into the mist of the morning with dim light breaking slowly around them. Happiness surged through them. Better than wine it was, because wine could make a man drowsy, and this made them eager for the day and whatever it might hold.

Chapter Four

CLOSE TO TWO months were behind them now, and the better part of their first two thousand miles on the Great Trace. Out of the home river they had gone into the Ottawa, paddling always against the current, then into the Mattawa; into Lake Nipissing they had paddled, and out of it into the French River where they were aided by a westward flowing current. Thirty-six portages had been made in all, the last and longest by the sault at Saint Mary's River where the roar of the rapids drowned even their imprecations. Once they were in the great lake and heading for their rendezvous with the other nine canoes of the brigade, they had less than four hundred miles to do, and the men laid bets with each other as to whether they would do it in four days or five.

"Five," Martin parried, for even that would mean hard and constant going, with everything in their favor.

One day had been so like another, one night so like the preceding, that for Guillaume the time had merged into an experience through which his confidence had gained deep roots. He had never doubted his ability to sing; he had had to learn that he could paddle and portage like a seasoned voyageur and use pipes and poses to his advantage. Only

48

the weather had made one day different from another, but neither rain nor fog nor wind had caused them to lose a single day; fair skies had been their boon more often than not. And "Pourquoi pas?" the men asked each other. They had put themselves at the start in the keeping of their patron saint, and she never failed her own. If storms or rough water had been their lot, they would only have prayed more and paddled harder. They would not have doubted for a moment Ste. Anne's ability to bring them safely to their destination.

Early in the afternoon of the third day out from the sault at Saint Mary's, the brigade met at an assigned place at a large sheltered cove. Open fields framed by woodland sloped down to the water. Two canoes had already arrived, and others kept coming during the course of the hours until all ten were accounted for. Greetings were warmly given, and the cooks vied with each other to create a banquet quite other than the fare on which the men had lived since they had set out from Lachine. There were fish in the lake for the catching, game in the forest for the hunting, and there was time; for once there was plenty of time. Twilight did not close in on these late June evenings until nearly ten o'clock, and a moon riding near the full just then would make night negligible.

When the feast was ready, a keg of high wine was opened and every voyageur was given his share. It was only after they had feasted and were sitting around the one big fire that the men of the different canoes began to tell of the adventures that had befallen them since they had set out on the May morning that, to many of them, seemed a lifetime away. Some of the stories were of actual experiences, and these were soon told; the best stories were of dangers encountered that bordered close to disaster, not for one man alone but for the canoe and its cargo. But always the danger was overcome, the disaster averted, and possible death outwitted. A voyageur honored the crosses he saw along his march, and prayed fervently for the peace of different souls while knowing that his paddle would not have been surrendered at that particular place nor would he have let his proud calling down by the folly of dying.

Laurent, bowman in the Number Five canoe, was a great storyteller, and whether he told of what happened two weeks ago or two years ago never mattered in the least.

"Ah, there was a time when I was a fool," he began sadly, as he asked for sympathetic listening after the high wine had gone around for the third time.

"How so?" one of his canoe comrades prompted.

"I fell from my canoe and struck my head on a rock. When I floated upon the surface of the water, face down and arms like this"—he held his arms limply at his sides— "my comrades knew that I was dead. But the shore was too rock-strewn even for a shallow grave, and they did not know what to do with me. A dead man cannot be carried in a canoe nor can he be left lying on the water."

"Pourquoi pas?" the words trembled on Guillaume's lips, but there was no sound behind them.

"But then"—and Laurent's voice quickened, his eyes danced as they roved around the group to make sure that every man's attention was on him—"a canoe bound for Lachine came along, carrying a keg of high wine with no more than an inch remaining in it. In less time than it takes a woman to change her chemise, they had put my poor limp body into that keg and sent it on its way to Montréal along with all the furs! Eh bien, what did my good wife do when they brought it to her door but send for the priest and arrange for a funeral."

A gasp circled the group by the fire. Those who had heard the story and those for whom this was the first telling were equally eager for its conclusion.

"I can tell you that when I heard the priest starting to pray over me, I set up such a knocking from inside the cask that they were obliged to open it and, holà, out I rolled! The better for high wine than water, and none the worse for the rest save that my mustache was entangled with my legs and had to be cut free with a carving knife."

The men rolled on the ground in laughter at Laurent's tale.

Guillaume nudged Prosper. "Surely that is not true?"

"Peu importe? It is as good a story as you will hear tonight and it well may be the last."

Laurent watched the men; then, in deference to them all, he said reverently, "Ah, a voyageur does not die easily."

Prosper was right about its being the last story. No one could better it and no one would dim its luster with a lesser tale, so the men soon sought their resting places.

The sun was well up in the sky when the cooks gave their familiar "Alerte, lève, lève nos gens!" and the men partook of their usual rations, then went to their work of loading the canoes. During the time that their march lay along the shore of the great lake, they would be in sight of each other if a storm did not arise to cause havoc; but they would not camp together again, as the coves along the rocky shore were too small to accommodate more than one canoe at a time. The various steersmen determined a meeting place in the lake three pipes out from Grand Portage; then they set off, one at a time and in numerical order.

"Demain ou l'après-demain?" the men demanded. "Tomorrow or the day after?"

"Peut-être," Martin replied. Rarely would he commit himself to an actual moment of time.

On the great lake it was different from the rivers and smaller bodies of water over which much of their journey had been made. Here there was a world of water around them, and the only shore to be seen was the one on their north along which they paddled; but if the water was calm and the sky favorable they would paddle far out into the lake to shorten their distance. As they did so, the shoreline faded until it was all but invisible. Water and sky surrounded them, still water, blue sky. When a breeze came up it was a sign that the Old Woman might be charmed into serving them. The mast that had not yet been used was raised, and one of the big covering sheets was attached to it. Only Martin and Henri kept their paddles in hand; the other voyageurs rested against the pièces while the wind did their work. Some of the men closed their eyes dreamily; others took from their beaded pouches pinches of tobacco, which they tossed into the water as an offering to the Old Woman.

"Souffle, souffle, La Vieille," they murmured respectfully.

Guillaume began to sing *Le Tambour*, but softly, softly, for the Old Woman could only be coaxed, and too hearty a demand might cause her to blow across the canoe rather than behind it.

> " 'Ra raderida
> Donnez-moi vôtre fille!' "

The men came in on the chorus, but softly too, holding back their strength for the time when it might be needed.

La Vieille began to fill the sail, puffing it out like the plump cheeks of her blowing. The men shifted their positions to feel the wind at their backs, sitting up to rest against it, then leaning back again on the pièces. So they sped along most of that entire day, and when they moved in toward the shore for the night they had gone almost twice the distance that they would have done with paddles. Martin studied the shoreline.

"Bien, mes voyageurs, très bien," he said. Not a single pipe had been called, for the day had been one long pipe.

Yet, when the canoe was beached and unloaded, the men had no desire to indulge in their usual games while supper was cooking. The day had been too easy, and something had been missing from it. They would not want many such days.

"We are ahead of ourselves, thanks to La Vieille," Prosper said to Guillaume, "and that is all to the good, for one never knows when the weather may take a day from us."

Hyacinth prepared supper even more quickly than usual; then he prepared for his other office, that of barber. Near the fire, though its glow was scarcely needed for the evening was long and light, the men lined up. Everyone wanted to have his hair cut to meet the collar of his shirt; some of them wanted to have their mustaches trimmed. All of them felt the need to make a good impression when they arrived the next day at Grand Portage.

Looking at Guillaume pityingly, Hyacinth curled his fingers over the boy's face where his mustache would someday be. "Give it time," he said, and there was comfort in his words; "it will come."

After his hair had been cut, Guillaume left the group

by the fire who were still awaiting Hyacinth's attention
and joined the men who had gone down to the shore and
were washing their shirts and breechcloths, trusting more
to the warmth of their bodies to dry them than to the air,
which already had the dampness of the evening in it.

The smooth far-reaching water of the lake was stained
blood red by the sunset. Voyageur after voyageur wagged
his head sagely as he watched the color deepen, then fade,
then gradually disappear. "Dieu merci," one after another
said, for a sunset like that meant only one thing: a day that
would be warm and fair, a day that would bring them to
safe haven.

"Tomorrow," Prosper said, "we will be with people again;
we can find shrift for our souls from the priest; we can go
to mass; but tonight it is as if we had seen le sang du
Christ poured out upon the water for us."

"You pray well, Prosper," Hypolite commented.

"I know what this journey can be," Prosper replied. "I
know that this time it has been good and I am thankful."

When morning came, the sun pointed a finger of light
through the mist that lay over the water. Gradually the
mist dissolved, and the finger became a path reaching into
the direction in which they would be traveling.

"En avant!" Martin called, and they were off.

With neither current nor wind to contend with, and
only calm water, they made good paddling time. Barring a
sudden fit of temper from La Vieille, they would easily
arrive at Grand Portage before the sun began its descent
behind the wooded hills. Near noon, and during the third
pipe, the brigade began to assemble on the broad blue
water. Words were exchanged among the steersmen, plans

made, and when the call came to go forward they knew that they were on the last lap. Another pipe was called after an hour, then another after they had rounded Point au Chapeau and could see the small settlement of Grand Portage ahead of them, south of where the Pigeon River came tumbling down from the hills and into the lake.

As they got nearer, they could see people coming down to the shore to welcome the brigade. Against the blue field of the sky fluttered a smaller field of blue, the Fleur-de-Lis, as much the flag of New France as of Old. The voyageurs hailed the sight and shouted a "Bravo!" that carried thinly across the distance to the people on the shore; then they crouched low and waited, each man for the word from the steersman in his own canoe.

The bowman in the Number One canoe fired a gun; from the shore came an answering boom. The steersmen shouted to their men, "Allons-y!" and the canoes shot forward with a burst of speed that had not been seen since their start in the waters above the rapids at Lachine.

"Chantez, Guillaume Puissante, chantez!"

Guillaume began one of the bravest and gayest and best known of all the songs, *Alouette!* One canoe after another in the brigade picked up the refrain, and soon all the men were singing, not the chorus alone but the simple enumerative words of the song itself that had been known and sung since childhood and that were always sung at the dash at the end of a voyage. When the many known verses came to an end and there were still several canoe lengths to be covered, Guillaume began improvising. The men had to listen then, but as if the enforced halt to their

singing only increased their power they came into the
chorus:

> " 'Alouette,
> Alouette,
> Ah!' "

with more volume and vigor than ever, and a force that
carried through to their paddles and increased the speed of
the canoes.

So singing, a hundred and forty voices strong; so paddling, a hundred and forty red-tipped paddles flashing in
unison, they covered the last part of their journey and
came into port.

"Arrêtez!" Nine canoes rested on the water, paddles
holding them steady, while the Number One canoe moved
up to the landing stage. Only after the men had leaped out
and the cargo had been stacked on the shore, the canoe
beached and turned on its side, did the Number Two
approach; then the next and the next until all ten were out
of the water. The pièces that had filled the canoes made a
small mountain on the shore; the provisions, now nearly
exhausted, took up little space.

Amid the welcoming crowd was the agent of La Compagnie Pelleterie. The steersmen from the different canoes
went up to him, clasped hands with him, then followed his
lead to the wooden building where lists would be checked.
While this went on, the men shouldered the pièces carried
by their various canoes and transported them to the building that served as warehouse, store, trading post, and
general shelter. There was much chatting and laughter as
the voyageurs met the people of the settlement, the traders
and trappers, the Indians and half-breeds. Dogs and chil-

dren darted among the crowd to see what morsels of food or attention might come to them.

After all the pièces had been deposited, there was one more task before the men were free for their fling. Each canoe must be thoroughly inspected, as each one had been at the end of a day's march. Repairs were made promptly from a kettle of bubbling pitch hung over a small fire near the mouth of the river; then a cordelle was drawn across all ten canoes so the wind could not tumble them, and the ends of the line were fastened to stakes in the ground.

Prosper stroked the keel of the Number Three canoe tenderly. "Rest well, mon ami, until we come back to you."

"It will be long?" Guillaume asked.

"Two months or a little less." Prosper shrugged his shoulders. "When we return from the pays d'en haut with the furs, the big canoes will carry us back to Montréal."

Hyacinth joined them, then Nicolet; then they joined others of the brigade, and went toward the wooden building.

"You may loosen your sashes, mes gens," Hyacinth reminded them, "for soon you will be eating such a meal as is a voyageur's due when he brings his craft safely to port."

They ate and drank and replenished their beaded pouches with tobacco from the supply the company agent had and gave to them freely. As the long twilight came to an end and still more people arrived at the building, they gathered around the great hearth to listen to the tales the northmen had to tell and to give in exchange the news they brought with them. As the brigades arrived, with needed supplies and news of the world beyond the great lake and the intervening waters, the people grasped it as

starving ones would food. Since the previous August, when
the last canoes had left the pays d'en haut, there had been
no news at all. "How is it in Montréal?" they asked. Some
even went further and asked, "How is it in France?"

Many of the northmen were French and had been
wintering in distant outposts where the fur trade was rich;
many were half French; but all had a hunger to know of
what was happening in the world they had come from and
to which they might, though no one could ever say for
sure, one day return. So the voyageurs told all they could
of politics and trade, of the life in Montréal and Québec;
they gave fragments of gossip heard on the streets and in
the wineshops. Memory served them well and it was as
exact as could be expected, or that mattered, until the time
came when news of the world beyond Grand Portage was
less important than news of their journey to Grand Portage.

They vied with each other then as they told of the
treacherous rapids, of the storms more violent than any
seen before by man since he had lived on the earth, of the
nights they had paddled with only the light of the stars to
guide them, and then had gone on paddling when the sun
made day for them. Guillaume, listening wide-eyed, felt
that he learned more from the telling than he had from
the living of the past two months.

"But enough of our news," Martin made an abrupt end,
"how is it in the pays d'en haut?"

Guillaume strained his ears to hear what would be said,
for this was the unknown to him. He opened his palms
and closed them again, thrusting his hands into his sash as
if to hold for remembering, not the promise of portage
and paddle, but what they led to. From Martin's map he

knew it was a land of many lakes, more than most men could count, varying in shape and size; of deep forests inhabited by people whose ways were not those of the French, and of animals who carried wealth on their backs.

"Comme ci, comme ça. Things have been good; things have been bad," one of the northmen said, shrugging his shoulders until they touched the tips of his ears. "We have kept peace with the tribes, and they have brought us furs. What more do you need to know?"

Silence fell on the room, the first silence for more than an hour, and it lasted for the space of time that it took a man to draw three deep breaths.

"Rien de plus," Martin was willing to concede, so breaking the silence.

"Vive les Peaux Rouges! The Indians!"

"Bravo!"

"Hourra!"

The men started shouting, pulling off their caps and tossing them in the air. They had had enough of talk, and were eager to get on to something else.

"C'est bon," Prosper turned to Guillaume. "The pays d'en haut will be there when we get to it. Why waste time now with words about it?"

"But I would know—" Guillaume began.

Prosper laid a finger across his lips and winked slyly. "All in good time, mon ami."

The company agent snapped his fingers and called for a dance, beckoning a man with a fiddle to come to the center of the room.

Everyone in the room responded. Some found partners among the Indian women who had been entering the building all during the evening; others found half-breed girls ready for a bit of gaiety. Some voyageurs, lacking women, bowed with exaggerated politeness to their fellows and joined the dance. Prosper seized Guillaume's arm, and the two careened around the room until the agent called the name of a particular dance and the fiddler began to scrape out its tune.

The figures, at first, were more courtly than those of the dances the men had engaged in around their camp-fires; but gradually the tempo increased. As the dancers sang louder and quenched their thirst more often from the cask that stood in one corner, they danced faster and with more abandon. All that they had been through during the past weeks faded into the revelry of this one night; all that was ahead of them became as nothing. When it was safely behind them, there would be another such fling.

When they began to weary with dancing, they called for a song, "Guillaume, Guillaume Puissante, chantez, chantez!"

Two of them seized him as he went spinning by with a half-breed girl. They set him up on a table where only empty plates and a few remnants told of the feast that had been spread there.

Guillaume, laughing and panting, thrust his hands through his curly hair; then, placing them on his hips, he breathed deeply for a moment. "Mais oui, messieurs et mesdames," he said, bowing low and turning his head to include them all, "what will you have me sing?"

With the prospect of a song before them, the revelers sought comfortable places for rest while a few slipped out of the door for the freedom of the night. Some curled up against the piles of pièces; others stretched out by the still-warm hearth; those with amicable partners found corners where there was no light to discover them.

"Que voulez-vous, mes amis?" Guillaume asked again.

Sounding almost like the chorus of one of the paddling songs, they shouted, "De l'amour! Chantez de l'amour!" The words came from voices thick with sleep, heavy with wine, but belonging to men who were more at ease than they had been for a long time.

Guillaume sang to them *Le Miracle du Nouveau-Né* tenderly, with all the sweet wistfulness that he could command and that the song deserved. He sang the fifteen verses, each one with its sentimental refrain, and by the time he came to the end he saw that most of his listeners were asleep. He was relieved, for the song was so sad in its end that it could bring tears to the eyes of the singer and grief to the heart of the listener; but there was comfort in it, too, as it told of the child newly born whose mother cared so little for it that she drowned it in the sea, yet whose soul was welcomed as it went to Paradise by angels three and angels bright. He did little more than whisper the last refrain as he got down from the table:

> " 'Je suis jeune; j'entends les bois retentir;
> Je suis jeune et jolie.' "

He moved like a shadow away from the guttering candles, past the hearth whose embers were cooling. As he placed his hand on the door, he glanced back at the room full of people, all of them taking their rest as a litter of puppies after a strenuous playtime.

"Dormez bien," Guillaume breathed to them. Dawn was not far off, and no day dawned that did not mean work.

Sleep was heavy on him, too, but when he opened the door the rush of night air, damp and cool as it came in from the lake, refreshed him momentarily. Aware of his own aloneness, he stood on the threshold uncertainly. As his eyes became used to the darkness, he saw the figure of one of the Indian women who had been part of the gaiety. She was leaning against the doorframe, more asleep than awake. At sight of him she lifted her arms, then made as if she would cradle him in them. It would have been easy, Guillaume thought, to fall into those outreaching arms. But lonely as he was, he could not sell his dream of love so soon.

"Pardon, ma vieille," he said gently as he went past the woman and toward the shore where the huddled canoes offered their shelter.

Tired as he was, sleep did not come soon; so he tightened his sash and sat by the canoes, listening to the sounds of the night—the ceaseless lapping of water on the pebbly shore, the occasional call of a loon, the whisper of wind in the distant forest. All was still in the building behind him, and in the few dwellings that made up the settlement. He began to sing quietly to himself, realizing as he did so how impossible of attainment was the love of which he sang: princesses waited in rose gardens for their cavaliers, shepherdesses in flowery meadows for their returning soldiers. This was not for him, nor would it be for anyone in New France, yet singing of love as he had for so long he had created for himself an image of the one to whom he would give his love. She would be fair, with blue eyes and hands whose caresses would be as tender as the kisses from her lips. In the eye of his mind he saw her, and she was real to him there. He would tell his dream to no one, but wait for it to appear.

The words of Monsieur le Comte crept across his dream, "Le seul péché c'est de trahir l'amour." If he did not wait, he might be guilty of that one sin. Looking up into the starry sky, it was as if he saw her face, but not clearly; yet he knew that when he met her he would know her. Until then he would sing of love. The position of the stars told him that there was little left of the night, but there was no hint of morning yet along the eastern shore of the great lake.

He went to the Number Three canoe and removed his bundle of possibles from its place under the thwart. Unfolding his capote, he wrapped it around him and crawled beneath the canoe. The song he had been singing faded from his lips. Sleep held him in its undemanding arms.

Next morning, and for most of the week that followed, all was hustle and bustle in the warehouse as the pièces were placed on the long plank tables, unpacked and reassembled. More and more Indians began to arrive from the north country with their furs, and the air rang with the business that ensued. Interpreters mingled with company agents and voyageurs as prime pelts were set beside tawdry trinkets and reasonably fair exchange was made. What meant little but work on his trapline to an Indian was the wealth of the fur trade to a Frenchman; a handful of beads that might be worthless to a Frenchman could be valuable to an Indian for his own wear or as barter with remote tribes.

As the packing of the trade goods proceeded, men were assigned to the smaller canoes that were waiting at Pigeon River. Martin and Henri were given six of their original crew—Hyacinth, Prosper, Guillaume, Hypolite, Nicolet, and Michel. The others were assigned elsewhere but would be waiting at Grand Portage when the journey back was to be made. Packs were reassembled in the familiar ninety-pound pièces with merchandise for specific posts in the pays d'en haut according to the needs and tastes of the Indians with whom trade would be made. Outer wrappings were marked with vermilion signs. Provisions were allocated, and all that remained was the portaging to the waiting canoes.

Chapter Five

IT WAS A hot July day when Martin's men started over the nine-mile portage to avoid the many falls on the Pigeon River. The air was swarming with insects. Dark cloud masses hung low over the lake. Song might have helped, but there would be no singing on this part of the journey, for a man needed every breath he could draw to keep him going uphill with two ninety-pound pièces on his back. Each man was responsible for getting eight pièces over the portage. Two at a time was customary, and two trips a day if there was no rain to make the going slippery. Three trips a day was not impossible, and the voyageur doing that earned an extra Spanish dollar, which was paid him at the time. Pack animals had been tried on the portage, but no animal with four feet to account for had ever been able to do what the voyageur could with his sharp eyes, powerful shoulders, and agile steps.

Prosper stood beside Guillaume as they waited to have their loads put on their backs. Henri and Martin had already gone ahead, up the narrow, rocky trail, each one bent almost double under his two pièces, the first fastened to the back by means of a broad leather collar, the second fastened by means of a tumpline that went across the forehead and took some weight from the back. Both pièces were lashed tightly together and to the man who carried them, for a loosely bound load could cause loss of balance. A slip might mean injury or loss of time.

Leaning into his load, and ready to follow the others away from the warehouse and on to the portage, Prosper turned ever so slightly to Guillaume. "Mon ami, you will take one pièce only."

"But, Prosper, I am a man. I can accept two."

Prosper said no more.

When the agent who was loading the men secured a pièce to Guillaume's collar, he said, "Ça va," and gave Guillaume a slap on his buttocks.

"Ça va," Guillaume replied, and set off, trotting as he saw the other men do.

The first thousand feet up Mount Rose, miles from the tumbling, chattering Pigeon River were the hardest; once accomplished, a voyageur had proved to himself that he could do the rest. Pride and strength were equally balanced.

Sixteen poses marked the distance from Grand Portage to the terminus. At no one did a voyageur release himself from his load; at no one did he even reach for his pipe. Leaning his hands and his weight against a tree and breathing hard, he let such rest come to him as would, and was ready to trot on again when the allotted time had elapsed. Few words were exchanged, for breath was precious. Although Guillaume could not sing, he found much diversion on the path itself. The moccasined prints of his comrades' feet were not the only impress on the soft earth. Crossing the path at one place were the cowlike prints a moose had made, and at many places were the cloven marks left by deer. Once, when he leaned forward against a tree at a pose, he saw the unmistakable scratching of a bear's claws in the bark.

At the strand at Pigeon River the canots de nord were waiting. These canoes, shorter by ten feet than the Montréal canoes, and narrower by a foot, could accommodate eight men, more than a ton of merchandise, and the usual complement of supplies and provisions. As they bobbed on the water, the canoes looked light and fragile, but their aspect changed as they were loaded—each one as carefully, and under the supervision of its steersman, as the larger ones had been at Lachine under the watchful eye of Monsieur François. Many of the canoes had designs on their prows—birds, animals, curious symbols. Martin pointed to the canoe that bore a full-faced vermilion sun on its high curved prow, and indicated that it was to be theirs. The men began loading it with the pièces they had portaged and deposited on the strand.

Twenty canoes had already taken off to the shouts and cheers of whatever voyageurs had been present. Each one had its own destination: some distant outpost in the world of lakes and rivers where its merchandise would be exchanged for furs. They might see one another in the course of the summer. If on an open lake, one canoe would race another and do all in its power to overtake and get ahead before the next portage; or, if bound by wind or heavy rain, two canoes might share a camping place for a night or until the weather freed them; but any meeting would be by chance and not arrangement. Some groups would rejoin at Grand Portage; all would meet in Montréal before the winter set in.

"Or in heaven!" Hypolite called cheerfully as a canoe was pushed away from the strand.

"Mais oui, au ciel! au ciel!" the men shouted gaily, for that was the one place where a Frenchman could be sure of being reunited with his friends.

The canoe with the full-faced sun lay in the water a few feet from the shore, heavily loaded. Guillaume, Prosper, Michel, Hyacinth, Hypolite, and Nicolet waded out to board it. Sitting in their places, they held the canoe steady with their paddles resting on the sandy bottom while Henri jumped in to take his seat in the bow and Martin stepped over the gunnel to stand in the stern.

"The last to leave," Martin said, as he looked around him and ahead to the canoe that was disappearing in the distance, "we may be the last to return. We have a long way to go." His eyes rested on the men crouched in position, on the load; then he called the words they were waiting for, "En avant!"

Now that they were off at last on the northwest road, heat, insects, toil all seemed behind them as they skimmed over the surface of the Pigeon River. Paddles moved steadily, voices rang cadently in *En Roulant Ma Boule*. Relief that work could be done again by eight men together instead of by individuals shouldering pièces over a portage gave them new energy.

"Ah, this is good! This is the best!" Prosper exclaimed when the singing came to an end and they had stopped for their first pipe. He moved his left hand in a wide arc that embraced the shining blue of the water, the distant granite wall of a cliff that dropped sheer to the blue, the near shadow where the forest reached down to the water.

Though summer days were long, summer itself was short, and a leeway of time had always to be allowed for the unexpected. Martin asked nothing of the men that they were not willing to give. A journey of eighteen hours on a clear day over calm water could see them close to a hundred miles on their road; a lesser march might be necessitated because of long portages or enveloping mist, the worst kind of weather for a voyageur. Days of gently falling rain were Ste. Anne's way of blessing her patrons, rain that was not heavy enough to swamp the canoe but rain that kept off the hordes of mosquitoes, cooled bare skin, and refreshed parched lips. When clouds hung low over the trees and dampness was in the air, Martin called for a pipe. As the canoe lay at ease, the men took off shirts and caps, and folded them under their seats to keep them dry. Then, lifting their paddles in welcome and thanksgiving, they bent to their task while the rain ran over their heads, down their backs, and blessed them. One of the middle men was ready to use the sponge that was part of their equipment if the rain started to collect below the poles on which the canvas-bound pièces rested.

A day's march had its fill of smooth water and rough, and after it the voyageurs around their campfire had a way of shrugging off its achievement with the simple, familiar exclamation, "Moi, je suis un homme!" To be a voyageur was to prove oneself a man and so to glory in a common birthright. Listening to them, Guillaume's thoughts often went back to the summers he had spent with his mother's people. The tribe lived not so deep in the wilderness as he was now, but deep enough so that his environment had been one of lakes and rivers, tall guardian trees, wild creatures of woods and water, and brooding silence. He had not thought back to the tribe often during the years of his growing at the château, but now the life seemed near him. Memory surged through him with such force that he felt himself to be more a part of his early life than of his later one.

He had left the tribe soon enough to make his first communion as a French child should; he had left it too soon to have established his manhood in his own eyes and in those of the braves as an Indian must do. Whenever he heard the proud boast, "Moi, je suis un homme!" he felt that something unaccomplished hung over him.

He did not know what precisely would have been asked of him in the tribe as a test of manhood, as it differed with each individual. All had to go apart for a period of time, alone, without fear, and accepting help from no one. All had to prove by their safe return that they had been able to defend and provide for themselves. But he had left too soon, and his right to manhood had not been established among his mother's people.

Perhaps it was as well, he reflected, for he had never wholly belonged to them; nor had he ever wholly belonged to the life at the château. Yet, he reminded himself, had he remained with the tribe he would never have learned all that Monsieur le Comte had taught him. He would not have learned to sing. He would not have known what it was to dream—to say, "Ah!" and close his eyes, since for what was seen inwardly there were no words. This last reminder prodded him sharply, for a man without a dream was only a portion of a man. "Moi," he whispered the words to himself, "moi, je suis un homme." Someday he would be able to shout those words.

No night was ever long now, as Hyacinth invariably called them to arise by three o'clock, and even before the first light thinned the darkness they had had their meal, loaded the canoe, and were off. One morning, even in the half-light, Guillaume could see that Henri and Martin, Prosper and Hyacinth, were wearing long-barred feathers in their red caps. Guillaume pointed to them.

Prosper laughed, "You will be wearing one by night, as will Hypolite and Nicolet and Michel. Wait and see, mon ami."

By midday they came to rest at the Height of Land Portage that lay between two lakes. Martin, with gestures and words, helped Guillaume and the others who had not been beyond Grand Portage to understand that from this point the waters behind them flowed back into the great lake over which they had come. "The waters before us flow north into a body of water that is so vast men once thought it to be the Western Sea. We do not go that far. That is where the English have their posts and their trade with the Indians."

No one made any comment. It was neither the time nor the place to discuss rivals in the fur trade. All that concerned them then was to bring the canoe in without grazing bottom or sides. When this was done, they fastened it securely to a tree; then the four men whose caps were featherless were told to stand on the shore to receive their baptism.

Henri had already cut a short cedar bough that he dipped in the water; then Martin sprinkled it over the heads of the four and asked them to repeat certain words after him.

"I, Guillaume, Hypolite, Nicolet, Michel, do most solemnly say that I will never allow a new voyageur to pass this place without giving him his baptism."

After Martin, the four repeated the words.

"I, Guillaume, Hypolite, Nicolet, Michel, do solemnly

promise that I will never aid my rivals in any way but work with all my powers for the company that has engaged me, La Compagnie Pelleterie."

Again they repeated the words.

"And now, most solemnly do I promise that I will never kiss the wife of another voyageur against her own free will."

The reply to this was given heartily, with a sly winking of the eyes at their comrades.

Martin sprinkled them again with water from the cedar bough, and Henri came toward them with four feathers, long and gray and barred, like the tail feathers of a hawk and similar to those the four earlier baptized men were sporting. Henri affixed each one carefully to a red cap, then kissed the owner of the cap on both cheeks.

"Now, you are true voyageurs; you have earned your feathers!"

While the ceremony was going on, Hyacinth had gathered wood for the fire and begun his preparations for their meal. At a word from Martin, the canoe was beached, unloaded, upturned, and the men were given what remained of the afternoon for their own pursuits—fishing, hunting, swimming, washing their clothes.

"Tonight we feast in honor of les baptêmes," Martin said as he tapped the keg of high wine that had just been brought to him. "Tomorrow we enter white water."

Guillaume glanced at Prosper questioningly. Surely they had already been through much white water.

"Ah—" Prosper drew in his breath sharply, as if he had caught a savor of what was before them. He smiled exultantly and smacked his lips at the taste on them. "It is hard to wait."

That night, long after the feasting and storytelling were over, long after the men had given themselves to sleep, Guillaume lay awake. Beside him was his red cap with the feather. Touching it in the darkness, he whispered for the hundredth time, "Moi, je suis voyageur!" He had said those words in Montréal when he could not have proved them and only the saving grace of song had aided him. Now he had proof. One step at a time as one went up a portage trail, the next step would be his all in good time.

The Height of Land Portage was made during the first light the following morning, and by the time the light was full the canoe had been loaded and every voyageur was in his place, all of them wearing their feathers. The usual prayer before entering a new body of water was said; Martin released them to action with a command, and they were paddling to the time of *Il S'est Mis à Turlutter*. The brief, gay refrain suited their morning mood:

> " 'Digue dindaine,
> Digue dindé.' "

Many times during the day they sang that same song, not because of any particular feeling for the old grandmother who lamented the old grandfather devoured with his sheep by the wolves, but because the miraculous ending gave them the sort of confidence they needed. In the song, the one who tells it went tootling with his pipe through the meadows until the lost were found and returned; then the two old people took the sheep by their trotters and all danced a merry round.

> " 'Digue dindaine,
> Digue dindé.' "

As Martin had promised, they had much white water but few portages to make. The level of the lakes was unusually high because of abundant rain in the spring, and many rapids could be safely run.

At a sign from the bowman, Guillaume hastened his tempo when the canoe moved into swift and swirling water. In such places, the canoe had to be kept moving faster than the water in order that steering could be done effectively. The staccato refrain from *Il S'est Mis à Turlutter* aided the voyageurs in bearing down hard on their paddles. Once safely out of the plunging water, but still in its current, a shout would go up from every man. The current might have hold of their craft, but their paddles would hold it controlled. The shout was one not of relief but of sheer glee. One danger had been passed. Where was the next? Like an echo to the shout came the whisper of prayer: there, on the shore past which they were running, was a cross made from a broken paddle. Off came the red caps, but with care so no feather would be dislodged; heads were bowed, words murmured, then paddling resumed.

The force of the current had carried them well into the next lake when Martin called for a pipe. They rested on the shining water in the blaze of the sun; insects droning in the air around them sounded louder than the snarling of the rapids behind them. Prosper lifted his pipe and waved it, creating a circle of smoke into which insects did not come. "See, mon ami,'" he said, pointing his pipe far into the distance in the direction of an odd-shaped tree that stood against the horizon.

Guillaume nodded.

"It is the place, is it not, Martin?" Prosper asked without turning his head.

"Yes, in the second lake from here. It is the lobstick that marks our turn. After we pass it, we follow the river north."

The voyageurs looked at the tree, trying to estimate how many pipes it would be before they would reach it. It was as tall and straight a lob tree as any that ever marked a turn in the road. A spruce, sheared of its branches except those near the top, it was ungainly as a tree, but as a direction mark it told steersmen what they needed to know.

"It speaks of more than our direction," Henri added. "It tells us that we have gone half our journey into the pays d'en haut."

A sorrowful murmur came from the men in the canoe.

"But the summer is half over," Martin reminded them.

"Hélas!" The reminder brought expressions of regret from the men, but winter was still too far ahead for them to give it more than a passing thought.

"Two weeks to our destination," said Prosper, who had been over the road many times before, "and a week at the post, Martin?"

"Peut-être," Martin replied guardedly. "It depends how trade goes and whether the canoe needs much repair."

"Bien. Two weeks back to the lobstick," Prosper went on; "then I shall climb it and put my mark near the top. It will be the twelfth time for me!"

"Ho, ho," Hyacinth chuckled, "you are too old to climb that tree."

"Pardon, mon ami," Prosper said gently, for to turn his head or become emphatic might have disturbed the precarious balance of the canoe, "he who can hold a paddle can climb a tree."

"When I see, I believe," Hyacinth amended.

So bantering, while puffing the blue smoke from their pipes, the time passed.

"Mon chanteur," Martin said, and Guillaume raised his left hand to show that he was listening, "we do not sing until we are in the next lake, beyond the meeting of the waters. I know this passage well. We shall run it easily, but every man must be ready to follow Henri's lead and my command—right, left, bear down, lift. Eh, bien?"

"Bien," said the men, as if the word were the refrain of the song they would not sing.

"En avant!"

They paddled in their usual manner until a point of land was rounded and Martin told them to be on their watch for submerged rocks and unexpected eddies, for beyond the point the water coursed through a narrow channel that led into the next lake. The men, always vigilant, maintained their unified strokes and speed. The point of land was comfortably rounded, and once in the channel the course of the water bore them on and paddles were used only to hold their course to the middle of the narrow way.

High walls rose on either side, walls of pink granite streaked with white, overhung with moss, dotted with orange and gray lichen. No voyageur spoke; if he had, the sound of his own voice would have come back to him in muffled, ghostly tones. Only the whisper of the water could be heard as it ran past the sides of the canoe and as it resisted the angle of a paddle, only the breathing of the men. Many of the men who had been in the channel before remembered the story of the canoe that had gone through with every man singing; when their song ceased it had returned to them, and the sound was the voices of lost voyageurs giving their warning. But it had been too late. The canoe had been caught in the rapids at the end of the channel. Its men had fought bravely to save it; but swung from one side to the other by the force of the water, it had brushed a boulder, then spun like a top until it smashed into another. It sank in less time than a man could say his Notre Père.

The men of the sun-faced canoe would tell that story when they made camp that night on the small beach at the base of the lob tree. In the bright glow of their fire everyone could make sport of the danger they had run in silence; but while in its midst eyes would ever be on the water, lips would be shaping prayers, and paddle arms would be strong and ready to keep the canoe upright and on its course.

"Lentement," Martin said, as softly as if his words were breathed over a babe in a cradle. "Doucement."

Guillaume repeated the words, not with the tip of his tongue but with the tip of his paddle.

All paddles were turned, and speed was cut as the high walls of the channel were left behind the canoe and a series of rapids leaped before it.

"Hold!" Martin called.

The canoe was kept close to a standstill while Henri studied the course ahead. Deep breaths were drawn by the men in readiness for the brief battle that lay before them. Guillaume drew the air in so vigorously that he all but choked.

"Courage, mon vieux," Prosper whispered between his teeth. "Some of the smoothest water in all the pays d'en haut lies before us."

"But after—"

"Yes, after we find passage."

Henri's keen eyes read the water. On both sides of it along the shore were boulders around which the water curled and foamed, against which spume rose and dissolved. Near the bow's tip, a whirlpool laced with foam rocked the canoe with its movement. Beyond the whirlpool was a dark area where the current ran deep and swift. Free of any boulders, it led straight to the open water of the lake beyond. Henri studied the passage long enough to make certain that no rocks had shifted, that no danger lay submerged. Where there was moving water the canoe would be in its element. For sixty seconds, no less and, God willing, no more, they would keep the canoe to a forward course and the water would do the rest.

He raised his left arm and held it straight as an arrow before him, indicating the way through the open gate of the dark water to the wide expanse of the lake that gleamed in the sunshine before them. "Tout droit," he said, as if he were talking to the water, but every man heard his words and knew what would be expected.

"Tout droit," Guillaume repeated to himself.

Martin called out, "We shall run it easily. Now, mes voyageurs—avancez!"

Paddles were raised and bore down to cut the water. The canoe edged forward and into the whirlpool, into the gap between the boulders where the water ran dark and swift and without any foam on its surface. Guillaume watched the water, daring it to do its worst.

The force that could have made a cork of something uncontrolled caused the heavily laden craft to shudder. The bow veered to the left, then was straightened. The men leaned on their paddles, crouching so low that spray from the swirling water wet their faces. Guillaume bore down hard on his paddle. His tightly clenched lips parted, and through them came words he had been saving for just such an occasion. He laughed as he spat them into the water; then he leaned farther forward, and at that moment his paddle caught between bottom rocks. He struggled to free it. When the canoe shot on out of the whirlpool and into the swift-moving current, Guillaume Puissante went over the gunnel and was sucked into the water.

Eight men would have shouted with glee when out of the dangerous passage; seven men now cried out in anguish when they realized that one of their number had gone into the water.

"Guillaume! Guillaume!" they called, but the sound was a whisper in a whirlwind.

There was no stopping the canoe until the force of the current on which it rode had carried it well into the lake. They turned it, then, and paddled toward the shore to get free of the current. They strained their eyes for a glimpse of their comrade in the water or on the shore. They called his name loud and long, hoping the sound of many voices would carry over the thunder of the rapids. Henri and Martin left the canoe while the others held it steady. They searched the south shore as far as the whirlpool. Standing near it, they shook their heads sorrowfully as their eyes probed the opposite shore, but so boulder-bound and water-whipped it was that no man could have made it to that shore, and lived.

First Martin, then Henri, pulled off his cap and knelt on the spume-wet rocks near the rapids to pray for Guillaume's soul.

"On our return we shall make a cross to mark his place," Martin said.

Henri took the feathers from their caps and crossed them together; then he laid them on the moss by the shore and held them down with stones. "Until then, this will serve."

They rejoined the canoe, waiting in the lake off the shore. There was no need to tell the others. Mournfully Prosper held up the handle of the paddle that had come down on the current. Again they prayed, for an hour had passed and no sign but the broken paddle had appeared. In his heart each voyageur was forced to admit that no man could have battled the current for more than a minute and lived; no man, not even Guillaume Puissante.

Henri and Martin, standing in the water, steadied the canoe while a pièce was shifted to equalize the weight. Prosper moved toward the center of the thwart on which he and Guillaume had sat, and as he did so he was aware of the folded capote in which were Guillaume's possibles. He covered it with his hand to make sure that it was safe. There it would stay for the time. He would be the one responsible for it, and at the end of the summer he would return it to Monsieur Bénédict. A steersman's paddle was handed to Prosper so he could use it first on one side, then the other. To be short one man in a north canoe meant that each voyageur would have to work that much harder; to be short a voice such as Guillaume's was the greater deprivation.

"Le bon Dieu must have need of him in heaven," Nicolet said, trying to comfort the others.

"Sacré bleu!" Prosper exclaimed, for sorrow had made him short tempered. "There must be many angels who can sing. Le bon Dieu might have spared him to us a little longer."

Avoiding the current as best they could, they paddled along the shore for one last look. Near the meeting of the waters, where the rapids flowed into the lake, they peered up the long channel where ghostly voices were said to linger. No one would have been surprised had Guillaume's voice been heard then, even above the din. Following Martin's commands, they turned the canoe carefully, moved toward the current, and so rode on it into the broad lake. As they paddled, they sang to lift their spirits, though no man had heart for his song; they sang in memory of their lost comrade.

In the split second when Guillaume realized that his paddle was caught and that he must either forfeit a voyageur's proud possession or go in after it to release it, he was conscious of only one need, and that was to fill his powerful lungs with all the air he could before he went under. Once in the water, he wrestled with the wedged paddle until it broke in his hands: the handle floated to the surface; the blade remained caught between rocks. The churned and racing water was so murky that Guillaume could see nothing, and the sound of it deafened him. Rocks, shifting in the stream bed, rolled against him. His store of breath was rapidly becoming exhausted, and he knew that he must surface. Only then was he aware of the undertow that would not let him surface.

As suddenly as everything within the last few seconds had happened, he was a child again, swimming with the other children, earning for himself the name Brother-of-the-Beaver. He did what he had done then: crawled along the stream bed until he was away from the current and free of the sucking power of the undertow. Moments later, exhausted and gasping for breath, he pulled himself up on the shore and lay face down, panting, spitting out mouthfuls of water. As his fingers dug into the duff, the realization came over him that his right hand was empty. Sick at what he had done in losing his paddle, shamed by his folly, he mustered the strength to crawl farther ashore to hide himself in a small clump of bushes. There was a roaring in his head louder than that of the rapids a few yards downstream of where he lay. Neither his arms nor his legs seemed to belong to him. He could not move; he did not want to move. No voyageur now, not even a man, he had failed his comrades as well as himself.

Distantly, as if the sound came from another world, he heard his name being called. He heard voices as of people in the forest not far from him, yet not near enough to discover him. He tried to speak, but no sound came; then shame swept over him again and he would not speak, even if he could. He heard the voices again.

"Il est mort."

"Si jeune, pauvre petit voyageur."

Then there were no more voices, only the sound of the water and the sound in his head.

A measure of strength began to return. He raised his head as if he were putting it into a tumpline that bore the weight of his body. Like the slowest of caterpillars, he inched his way over the forest floor, away from the rapids, over moss and twisted roots to the edge of the lake. Weak from the exertion of an hour and a distance of a hundred feet, he lay there. His wet clothes weighed on him, but he was without the ability even to shake himself as an animal would. He could raise one hand enough to reach his cap and pull it off. He looked at it and wondered where the feather had gone. Half of it was dark with a stain that was not water. Disgusted, and shamed yet more by the sight of his own blood, he tossed the cap away from him.

He raised himself again. Across the lake a broad band of light had been laid by the westering sun. In it his cap was floating, and in it, far away, something else was floating. His sight was blurred, but in his need to see he mustered the strength to shake his head, blink his eyes, and try to pierce the distance. He could not distinguish the object, but he could catch the sound that was coming from it: the faint sound of singing. He strained with every nerve to listen. The beat was not right. It would never call from men their best effort. It was too uneven, too hesitant. Pulling himself up to a sitting position, he tried to sing *À Saint-Malo* as it should be sung.

Try as he would, no voice came from him, only a mouthful of water still caught in his lungs. Because he had not the strength left to spit it out, it dribbled down his chin, over his chest, and onto his wet shirt. Wraith-like, the canoe went from his sight long before the singing that came from it was lost to his hearing. His head fell forward. Pain claimed his body, and weakness that he could not combat. But the agony in the pit of his stomach that made him want to curl into a knot to ease it and the rasping in his chest with every breath were as nothing to the throbbing in his head. He rolled sideways, glad for the pain in his body because it diminished the agony in his spirit. Around him the daylight world was going dark. Consciousness had little left to cling to.

"Notre Père," his lips shaped the words. The last ones

he would say on earth would place him in the hands of his Father in heaven. He opened his eyes for a moment. Lapped in the full light of the sun and wrapped in its warmth, he saw only a small area of light, but what there was was like an aureole. In it he discerned, faintly but unmistakably, the face of the one of whom he dreamed. It was fair, and it was smiling. Words from one of his songs sang themselves through him:

> "Je suis jeune; j'entends les bois retentir;
> Je suis jeune et jolie."

Then total darkness engulfed him.

Chapter Six

FROM A CLOUDLESS sky the sun poured light and warmth on lake and forest, as it would continue to do for another few hours; the water washed against the shore as it would do without regard for time. The canoe that had crossed the lake reached the far western end and, after unloading, was upturned on the beach at the base of the lob tree; but the red cap bobbed on the surface, hour after hour, moved less by the current than by the slight breeze that riffled the water; moved to a small pebble-strewn shore where the lake met the onrush of a stream; moved, now this way now that, until it caught the eye of an Indian who was searching the water bed for crayfish. He reached down and picked the red cap out of the water, shook it, then held it across the span of his palm and studied it. In another moment he had tucked it into his belt, left his occupation, and was running over the forest trail that bordered the stream to the place where a group of Indians had made a temporary encampment. There he placed it before his chief.

It was no mystery, a voyageur's cap. All the Indians of the region dealt in furs, and the voyageurs with their long canoes were the means by which furs were exchanged for needed goods; but it was well known that a voyageur did not part with his cap readily. Close fitting, it rested too snugly on his ears for him to lose it even in the wind; and he was not likely to give it away. The chief turned the cap slowly in his hands, as if it would somehow reveal of itself the reason for its appearance. He laid it down and took up his pipe; then, with eyes half closed and in slow deliberation, he smoked. Another brave came to join the one who had found the cap. Together they sat near the fire that smoldered in an ashpit before the lodge of the chief; an old woman and a girl who was scarcely more than a child stood near one of the great hemlocks that fringed the clearing. All waited for the chief's decision; all waited to see what significance a red cap had for them.

Once before, at the meeting of the waters, a heavily laden canoe had been swept under. There had been many caps then, and much plunder; but there had been sorrow, too. The high water this summer had made the passage navigable, and canoe after canoe had already gone over it, gone through the meeting of the waters and out into the broad lake, paddles flashing, voices singing.

At last the chief determined what should be done. He gestured to the brave who had brought him the cap and to the other one, calling them by name. He directed them to go to the easternmost end of the lake and search until they found the one to whom the cap belonged. "If he were lying on the bottom, his cap might still be over his ears and his spirit would have joined the Great Spirit. His cap came on the water, so somewhere he must be lying on the shore. If there is breath in him, bring him here. If there is no breath in him, bury him as these people bury their own and put two crossed sticks at the place."

Swift Arrow and Tall-as-the-Pine nodded assent.

Each one took an adz to use to cut through the earth and dislodge rocks if such was their need; each one took a paddle. They followed the trail to the shore, unslung their canoe from a tree in whose branches it had been slung, shoved it into the water, and set out. Their paddles made no sound; their craft left scarcely a ripple in its wake.

The light of the sun was long on the water, its rays deep gold, when the keen searching eyes of the two braves discovered the figure lying on the shore near the meeting of the waters. They beached their canoe and went toward the figure, shaking their heads silently, one of them making the gesture indicative that all was finished.

Guillaume lay, as he had for the past five hours, with his head on a patch of moss and his feet in the water. His moccasins and buckskin leggings were wet from the waves lapping constantly over and at them, but his blue shirt and breechcloth had been dried by the sun. His bare thighs and chest had drawn a host of flies and mosquitoes to them, as had the gash on his head where the blood had congealed. His sac-à-feu and his fur-sheathed knife still hung from his sash, but his pipe was gone.

Tall-as-the-Pine knelt beside Guillaume while Swift Arrow, standing near, did what he had seen the French adventurers do by the dead body of a comrade. He laid one hand on his breast, then moved the finger tips from brow to navel, from shoulder to shoulder. An Indian would have opened his hands in token of the spirit's release; a Frenchman preferred to use a charm, and the young man who lay on the shore was a Frenchman, though his skin was dark enough to be Indian and he carried no more flesh than he needed. Once this had been done, the brave put his hand on the beaded pouch and emptied its tobacco into his own pouch. What little there was was still wet, but it would dry.

The brave who was kneeling felt the hands, the brow; he put his head to the chest, his ear to the heart. After a long moment he glanced up at his companion. "There is life but it is faint, not a strong man demanding but a papoose whimpering. The sun has dried him since he came from the water, but it has not warmed him. He is as cold as a fish."

While he spoke, he untied the sash around the voyageur's body and slipped it from under the limp figure, careful to keep the knife attached. Working with practiced fingers, he wrapped the sash around the arms and fastened it so they would be close to the body; taking a leather thong from his belt, he did the same with the legs. This way it would be easier to carry the body to the canoe, and it would help conserve what little warmth was left.

One at the head, one at the feet, they bore the limp figure to the canoe and laid it in the bottom. By then the sun had dipped below the horizon and the lake was the color of a copper kettle. The canoe slid on to it and worked its way toward the pebbly shore at the mouth of the stream. Twilight was long, and what light it gave aided the two braves as they lifted the bound body from the canoe and carried it over the trail to their chief.

A pine knot was burning in the ground by the fire pit where the chief sat. He lifted his head when he saw the braves appear with their burden, then gestured toward a bed of spruce boughs at the base of a tree just beyond the circle of light. "Old Woman has made ready," he said.

After the body was laid on the boughs, the old woman accompanied by the young girl, stepped forward to minister to it.

Tall-as-the-Pine stood in front of the chief and made the zigzag upward sign for life. The gesture was made slowly, as if to indicate that the hold on life was a slight one.

"Old Woman knows what to do. Her hands have held many here," the chief said. "We leave at daybreak."

"The canoe is ready," the brave replied. "Tonight Swift Arrow and I sleep beside it." He motioned to the brave who was standing within the circle of light. Both left and melted into the darkness of the surrounding forest.

Old Woman knew at once that warmth was needed, warmth from without and warmth flowing within. With the girl's help, a buffalo skin that had been hanging from a branch above the bough bed was laid gently over the bound body. As the girl tucked it in at the sides and under the feet, Old Woman brought from the edge of the fire a container with liquid that had been kept warm in the ash. Drop by drop from the tip of her finger, she eased the liquid between the tightly closed lips.

When she was satisfied that enough had been swallowed for the time, she moved her hands under the buffalo skin to undo the sash that held the arms, the thong wrapped around the legs. As she did so, her fingers felt over the bones—arms, legs, ribs, chest, back, then rested on the heart to catch its beat. Informed about the condition of the body, she turned her attention to the gash across the left brow that extended into the hair above the ear. The girl followed Old Woman's monosyllabic commands and brought water and moss for the cleansing of the wound, then a piece of soft buckskin to place across it for protection. An hour had passed.

"Rest now," Old Woman said to the girl, who soon disappeared into the shadows. "Dormez bien," Old Woman whispered as she leaned over the face of the young voyageur.

The chief still sat motionless by the fire. Only when Old Woman approached him did he stir enough to acknowledge her presence.

She made the sign for life, then followed it with the sign for recover, turning her right hand across her breast and pointing upward; but instead of pointing with her first finger she used her little finger to indicate that the impulse within was small.

The chief nodded. "We leave at dawn. We return when the moon wanes. You will care for him until then."

Old Woman made a sound of assent. To herself she said, "I will care for him until he is ready to care for himself."

The chief rose from the circle of light and warmth and went into his lodge. Old Woman returned to sit beside the bough bed, to ease liquid from time to time between the lips that had now opened slightly, to feel the hands under the heavy buffalo skin and chafe them to encourage the returning warmth.

The smallest of smiles trembled over her lips as she observed the evidences of life—the flesh less cold, the breath coming more evenly. In a tone so low that it was scarcely more than the sound made by the flame guttering in the pine knot, she crooned a song that she had not thought of for many years, a lullaby. She had never given life, never bent over a cradle of her own, but more times than she could number she had held life within a wounded body, a sick body, until the strength had returned and life had again been able to rule its habitation. She knew now, as she had known on those other occasions, that deep sleep, dreamless sleep, was the beginning of the long road back to well-being. There was much the young man would soon have to do for himself, but his need now was for sleep, and that she could give him.

"Dormez, dormez bien," she whispered again as she came to the end of her song.

Sleep was for the young—the girl in particular, the chief and the braves who would leave at dawn with their furs for the trading post; such as she needed no sleep. She might nod, as she sat between the spruce bed and the ashpit; but if the young man made the slightest move she would be there to help him shift his position or to restrain him. She knew the French well enough to know that they sprang quickly from one thing to another, and with the wounded voyageur a swift action could undo much of the good that the long night's quiet was doing for him. Every now and then she reached over to touch him, gratified by the warm and living feel of his flesh.

When the gray of the first light filtered through the forest, she heard the grating of the canoe as the men pushed it into the water and knew that they were off with their load of furs. As the light increased, she studied the young man's face, pleased to see a faint hint of color in the cheeks but puzzled that there was no flickering of the eyelids. They seemed even more tightly closed, as if unwilling to be wakened by the day. The body had not been broken; of that she had made herself sure, though it had

been battered and bruised; it was the spirit that had suffered and that was hard to find and far harder to help. She
shook her head sadly. These men who powered the laden
canoes were as proud as they were strong; they boasted
that their lives meant little, that their work was all. For
them, pain of the body could be endured but not disgrace.
This one had been found without his paddle, without his
cap, and to a voyageur this was shame however it happened. Old Woman, reflecting on this with her eyes on
the impassive face before her, guessed that the young
man's hurt was deeper than any medicine she knew how
to brew could reach.

Guillaume gradually became aware of a faint crooning
sound. As he breathed, the aroma of newly cut spruce
titillated his nostrils; but what he heard and what he
smelled reached him as if both came from a far land, a
country other than the one he was in. Sound and scent
were comforting; they gave an ease that he had not known
for a long time, if ever, and he had no desire to break the
spell that brought them to him. Intrigued by them, he
began to wonder if they did come from far away or if he
was the one who was far away and they were the near
things. Whatever it was, he would not change the condition nor would he open his eyes to discover for himself.
He felt a weight upon him but it was a weight of warmth,
and that he would not change either, for he remembered
that he had been cold.

A long time ago, perhaps another lifetime ago, he had
been lying in the sun but it had had no warmth for him.
The shivering induced by the cold had driven pain through
his body, but he had not been able to control the shivering,
nor had the pain ceased until oblivion came. He felt

something being put to his lips. Wanting to resist it, he could not, for there was no fund of strength within him upon which he could call. Whatever it was that entered his mouth, it went down his throat without choking him, one drop at a time. He swallowed. Now the warmth that rested on him from without began to be met by a warmth rising within, a tide of warmth that seemed to creep through his entire body, seeking out its crannies of cold and dissolving them.

"You have need of more liquid?"

"No, it has done its work. There is a quickening. The beat of the heart is stronger."

"The men have gone?"

"Before the sun rose. I heard the canoe."

"The night has been long, Old Woman, and I have slept. Let me stay by the spruce bed while you rest."

"You speak well, Willow Wand. Stay now while I go."

Guillaume heard the voices, coming, like the other sensations, as if from a distant land; distant not only in space but in time, for they spoke in words that he had not heard since his early childhood.

There was movement near him. The slight pressure of a body as it knelt near the bough bed, the long fall of hair as it brushed across his face; then on his cheek just forward of his ear the impress of lips. There was silence, followed by a faint vibration from the forest floor as of steps in slow retreat. Light harassed his eyelids, but he did not want to open his eyes; he was still in a distant land. The thought of the long journey back wearied him so that he lost hold on consciousness and fell again into heavy sleep.

But not for long.

As light filled the forest and embraced him, he stirred under the weight of the buffalo skin. Realizing that he was in a far country, he began to feel an urge to find his way back to the place where he belonged. Weak as he was, and struggling to move even a little, his hands closed on a cordelle. It was a tracking cable made of many twisted strands of line, the kind used to haul a canoe over a sault. As long as he kept his hands on the cordelle, he knew that he could get back; for he was sure that the faraway land in which he was was not his own, no matter what ease and warmth it was giving him. His land lay at the other end of the cordelle and he must get to it, though it took all the strength he had.

Straining and losing his hold, then finding it and straining again he opened his eyes. At first he saw nothing but light that hurt without revealing; then he saw, dimly, the figure of a girl sitting near him.

She gave a cry of exultation, leaned forward, and touched his face with her fingers.

Guillaume tried to speak, but there seemed to be no sound within him. Even his lips failed him in shaping words.

The girl, as if to answer something she interpreted as a question in his bloodshot eyes, reached toward the ground and held up the beaded tobacco pouch and the red cap.

Guillaume stared at them, trying to read their meaning like a man trying to read the words of a language he had once known.

Willow Wand moved the two objects so he might see them more closely, and waited for him to speak.

"Non, non—" The words, thick, guttural, uttered with difficulty and accompanied by a slight movement of the head, were followed by a closing of the eyes and a sudden stiffening of the facial muscles.

Frightened, Willow Wand laid the pouch and the cap on the ground and ran into the forest to seek Old Woman.

Guillaume, once his hands had slipped from the cordelle, was back in his former state of semiconsciousness. What he had seen with open eyes had made him cognizant of his predicament and of his disgrace. Slowly, in a dream no longer but in bitter fact, he worked his way back over what had happened. He had been so sure that he could do everything as a true voyageur should; but he had let his paddle get caught, and in trying to release it he had broken it. A hot tide of shame ran through him, its current harder to battle than the current he had fought against in the water as he made his desperate effort to save himself. He could hear the rocks being rolled by the current; he could feel them thudding against his body. Suddenly, and much sooner than when it had actually happened, oblivion seized him. He could no longer swim against the current; he could no longer struggle to save his life. He could only let himself go into the darkness that had the power to blot out memory as well as pain.

Old Woman knelt beside the spruce bed and studied the face of the wounded voyageur; she reached under the buffalo skin to feel his hands. Her head was moving slowly from one side to the other. "I do not know whether we can bring him back again," she said.

The girl was perplexed. "When his eyes opened, Old Woman, I showed him his cap and his pouch. With one of my people a sight of his way of life makes him want to live again, but with him—no! It made him want to run from them."

"Willow Wand, you do not know these men as I do. They live by their pride. I can not tell you how this is, or why, but it was not good to show him those things. Put them away."

The girl looked up beseechingly. "You will do something?"

Old Woman nodded. "If we can find where pride still lives for him, he may come back to claim it. It is not in his present life. Perhaps in his childhood there was something—something—" She began to croon again, more to herself than to either of the others.

Succumbing to the darkness that was his world, Guillaume heard the murmur of voices near him, like wind whispering through the leaves of a birch tree, like lake water tumbling pebbles on a shore.

There was, in him, neither desire nor ability to indicate his slight awareness of the presence of others; even with the daylight full about him, there was no fluttering of the muscles in his eyelids. He had nothing to hold on to since the line his hands had closed over in the earlier dream had disappeared. One small flame guttered in his darkness: a wonderment within him that he understood their talk, for it was not French. It was the talk he had heard when he lived with the tribe, the talk of his mother's people. The image of his mother came into the darkness, and thinking of her made him a boy again, a boy in the deep green of the forest during the long summers when the ways of another people were as much his as were the ways of the French in the city that bordered the river. He gave a slight sigh, and his taut body relaxed against the spruce boughs.

The sigh was not unnoticed by Old Woman. She moved her head meaningfully. "Bring the dream net, Willow

Wand, and place it on the bough above his head. I go to prepare a medicine that will make him dream, but his dreams must be good or our work will fail."

While Old Woman sought out the roots she wanted and made a brew of them, Willow Wand placed the dream net on the nearest branch above the head of the sleeping voyageur. It might have been a spider's web, so cunningly was it made, and it was strong. A thin, narrow piece of ash wood had been curved and joined to form a hoop; then a network of fine threads had been strung across the five-inch diameter. The threads crossed in such a way that in the center there was a small opening, scarcely bigger than an eye. There was no sag to the threads, nor could any knots be seen. The girl studied the position of the net, then tilted it slightly by inserting a twig between it and the branch from which it hung.

Old Woman returned with her brew. Gently, from the tip of a finger she got what she felt was needed into the voyageur's mouth; then she rubbed his throat with her fingers to ease the swallowing. "He will sleep for a long time, and he will dream," she said, sure of her potion.

"And his dreams are guarded now," Willow Wand added, glad that she had been able to do something to make up for her earlier mistake. "Only the good ones will reach him."

They left, then, and each went her separate way to do her daily tasks.

Chapter Seven

ND DREAM GUILLAUME did, a dream that began far back in his childhood and brought him up to
a proud moment in his burgeoning manhood.

Among the children in the tribe there was one who,
though smaller than others of the same age, was like them
in all ways except that his black hair was soft and it curled
like strands of the ground pine. His skin was as brown as
the skin of the other children; his black eyes were as sharp.
He could run fast, swim hard, and climb to the top of any
tree. But, while the other children could chant of the
deeds done by their warriors, and tell strange tales of
animals that had been told to them, he could sing. They
called him Brother-of-the-Beaver because of his prowess
in the water; they might as well have called him Brother-
of-the-Birds.

He sang to them in another language until he put the
words into theirs, but what he could not put into their
understanding was of what he sang: sunny meadows where
flowers bloomed and sheep strayed away when a chevalier
came courting the shepherdess. What was a meadow? they
asked him. And what were sheep? Was a chevalier a chief?
He sang to them of saints going about their business on

earth while le bon Dieu prepared a place for them in heaven. Were saints medicine men? they asked him, and was le bon Dieu the Great Spirit? And heaven? What was that?

"Heaven? It is that world of light above us, but we can see it only at night through those peepholes we call the stars."

Even though there was much he could not explain to them, for there were many things he did not know, they listened to him because the sound of his voice was melodious and because through his songs they saw beyond their green forests and blue waters. He sang often of love, and when they asked him about it he smiled mysteriously. That was what he had seen Monsieur le Comte do when love was spoken of. With the hint that someday each one would know for himself, the question went unanswered.

The summers were long and warm and active; the winters were long and cold and quiet. One winter had been spent with the tribe; for all others he returned with his mother to the city and its hill, to the château and the comfortable kitchen, to the good rich food with sips from near-empty wineglasses, and to the times when he went up the winding stairs to the room where a fire of logs blazed and a man in a velvet tunic with lace at his throat and soft dark hair that curled to his shoulders was waiting. He was not Brother-of-the-Beaver then; he was Guillaume.

Monsieur le Comte held him on his knees and sang to him. He taught him new songs that Guillaume sang back to him.

"Faites attention, mon petit," he said. "Each word must be distinct." He shaped his lips, and the *o*'s came out rich and round; he shaped his lips again and the *r*'s trilled over them. "It is a courtesy to speak so one can be understood; it is an art so to sing. But more than the words, Guillaume, is the rhythm; that is the soul of the song. Listen—"

The boy watched and listened while the man sang one of the songs that had been sung by a troubadour in Old France many hundred years ago. Monsieur le Comte beat the measure with finger tips tapping on his knee, and after he had finished the boy did his best to sing the song back as he had heard it.

"Bravo, mon petit! It will come better in time."

Guillaume remembered the many long verses well, but against later forgetfulness Monsieur le Comte taught him how to write. With a quill plucked from a goose that had hung in the kitchen, and dipped in a silver inkwell that had come from France, Guillaume learned to make his letters and then to place them in words; he learned to make his numerals and then to arrange them in sequence. It was a proud day when he signed his name, *Guillaume*, with a flourish under it as Monsieur le Comte did. It looked small on the big sheet of paper until Monsieur le Comte wrote his own name under it: *Pierre de Puissante, Comte et Commandant*.

Into the warm room with the blazing fire, Monsieur le Curé came on occasions to instruct Guillaume in matters having to do with the Church. He told stories of the saints, and spoke of particular ones to turn to when lost or in trouble; he taught Guillaume prayers and gave him special ones to say when he was afraid or had sinned.

"What is 'sin,' Monsieur le Curé?" Guillaume asked.

Monsieur le Curé tried to explain, but Guillaume found

it as difficult to understand as the children of the tribe had found it difficult to understand when he told them about sunny meadows and flowers.

After the lesson, Monsieur le Comte and Monsieur le Curé had their glasses of wine, which they later gave to Guillaume to drain. They talked together, and he sang to them. As soon as Monsieur le Curé had left, Guillaume climbed onto Monsieur le Comte's knees and asked him about sin.

Monsieur le Comte was rarely at a loss for an answer to one of Guillaume's questions. He paused this time, then said, with the distinct enunciation he had been teaching the boy, "Le seul péché c'est de trahir l'amour."

Guillaume accepted the statement. He was wise enough in Monsieur le Comte's ways by then to know that that was all that would be said, not only today but on any other day, on the subject of sin. Whatever it was Guillaume asked le bon Dieu to forgive him for doing when he made his weekly confession would be taken care of by the words the priest said over him in Latin. Nobody understood them, but they worked their magic, as the chants of the medicine men in the tribe worked theirs. The world was full of things that could not be explained or understood.

"Peu importe." Guillaume shrugged his shoulders as he was learning to do. It mattered little.

Guillaume was to hear Monsieur le Comte say those words again the time he returned alone at the end of a long summer and climbed the stairs to the room where the fire blazed.

"Bienvenue, mon petit!"

It was the usual greeting, and in the way of years past Guillaume told of the summer, but there was much that he did not tell. The previous winter had marked a time of growing, and many of his friends were different. They had no longer wanted to listen to the songs he sang or play the games they had once enjoyed. The time had come for them to take their places as members of the tribe. By their actions when with each other and by their attitude toward him, Guillaume had been made to realize that he was not one of them. He had also been made to realize that he was not wholly one with the children who played in the streets of the city and around the gates of the château. Who was he, then? Alone that summer more than he had ever been before, he had tried to find an answer to his question. None of this could be put into words, but Monsieur le Comte sensed a withholding in Guillaume's story.

Taking one of the boy's hands in his, he held it. "You are growing, Guillaume; soon you will be mon petit no longer; but I shall not be here to see you become a man. I shall have returned to France by then."

Guillaume's heart plummeted like a stone cast into the water.

Monsieur le Comte's moods were mercurial, and in another moment he laughed as gaily as if their whole conversation had been one of pleasure. "But always we must go forward," he said. "It is not fit to be sad when there is so much to enjoy. Go now, and send the woman to me."

It was then that Guillaume told him he had returned alone to the city. His words were few. He did not speak of the brave who had been like a shadow behind his mother all during the summer, or of the heavy way his mother had walked on that last day in the forest.

There was a long silence, and this time it did not end

in laughter. "C'est ma faute," Monsieur le Comte murmured, beating his breast with his right hand in the gesture of penitence. Then, looking before him as if there
were no one else present and the words were for himself
or le bon Dieu, he had said, "Le seul péché c'est de trahir
l'amour." After another long moment he drew the boy to
him and placed his lips against his cheek. That was all.

Guillaume backed slowly away, turned, and went toward the door. Opening it without looking around, he left
the room and went down the winding stairs to the kitchen.
The words troubled him because he did not understand
them, but he would ask no one for their meaning. He
would not forget them. Like a talisman, he would take
them out of his memory from time to time and study
them; perhaps, someday, their meaning would be clear.

Several years passed, years of growing, years of wondering. Guillaume fitted into the life of a servant at the
château during all but the five summer months. That time
was spent in the forests and on the waters with companies
of soldiers or young adventurers come to New France. His
knowledge of the wild, his familiarity with one of the
Indian tongues, his tough, wiry body and ability to sing
made him useful in many ways. That he was not wholly
French or wholly Indian had ceased to bother him; he had
learned that he could use to advantage what each had
given him.

A few nights before *Le Cygne Chantant* was to sail back
to France with Monsieur le Comte among its passengers,
a banquet was given at the château, and Guillaume was one
of the entertainers. As the people at the long table feasted,
he waited for the time to come for him to sing. Always
impatient because of the delight he took in singing, he was

willing to be patient. For once he did not want the time to come too soon. All the songs he knew were ready to be sung, and his voice would not fail him; he had sung through enough feasts to know that. But all the songs he knew had been taught him by Monsieur le Comte, and after tonight he would never sing for him again.

"Allons! Allons!" Monsieur le Comte's voice rose above the babble in the hall. "Où est mon chanteur?"

Guillaume rose and approached, taking his position near the center part of the long table. He looked directly at Monsieur le Comte and, as invariably happened, the man's lips shaped the title of the desired song. Guillaume bowed; then, lifting his head proudly, he smiled at the gathered guests. Humming the tune through once, he drew to himself the attention of all at the table and gained the silence he required. *L'Hirondelle, Messagère de l'Amour* was the first of the many songs he sang.

His voice was high and clear. That it had lost its childish sweetness was not unnoticed by Monsieur le Comte, but in its place was a tone more substantial and a quality that presaged manhood. Song after song was called for, and Guillaume met the demands with merry zest. When he sensed that he had sung long enough, he returned to the first one; but this time *L'Hirondelle* was sung so softly that many at the table had to strain to hear. This was as it should be. The song was no more than an echo, a sign that the night was over. Glasses had been filled and drained many times; daylight was beginning to streak the windowpanes. Guillaume approached the table and bowed to Monsieur le Comte.

It was the custom in New France for the one who gave the feast to reach into his pocket and present the singer with a coin; but Monsieur le Comte went beyond the custom. He got up from his chair and left the table to stand beside the singer.

"Bravo, bravo, mon grand!" he said; then he drew Guillaume to him and placed his lips first on one cheek, then the other. He held them for a moment on the right cheek near the ear, sensitive to the down that had started to grow. Deep within him there was pride that the boy who sang so well was on his way to being a man, and a bearded Frenchman at that.

Chapter Eight

GUILLAUME PUT HIS hand to his face, as if to feel the benison he had been given. It was not his face that he touched, but the cordelle he had held before and of which he had lost hold. This time he knew that he must not lose hold, for his sole hope of return to the world in which he belonged was by the cordelle. The line that was strong enough to drag a loaded canoe safely through tumbling water could drag him out of oblivion. His grip tightened. Hand over hand, hand over hand, he hauled himself out of the darkness and into waking.

He opened his eyes slowly, naturally, willingly, as if to greet daylight after a night's long sleep, and took in his surroundings. He was in a forest and his hands were lying limp at his sides, as his body was limp under the weight of an animal skin. Near him sat an old woman with long dark hair, and dressed in a buckskin garment. She was not looking at him but in the direction where Guillaume heard a sound like lake water lapping. The clearing in which he lay was not large enough to be an Indian village; but it was clearly an encampment of some kind, for he could see, even without turning his head, a lodge made of boughs and the depression in the ground where a fire was being kept. Moving his head back ever so slightly, he saw, hanging directly over him, a dream net. He had not seen one since his childhood, but the mere sight of it gave him the comfort of the long familiar.

During the summers with the tribe, a dream net had always been hung above his sleeping place. This had been true for all the children, even to the papooses bound to their boards. He had accepted it as belonging to the night, as his small bow and quiver of arrows had belonged to the day, and under it he had felt safe. Of the dreams that filled the night, only the good ones could get through the hole in the center; the fearsome ones would be caught in the crisscrossing strands and held fast to be shriveled into nothingness when the first light of morning found them. Sleep was safeguarded, not by the dream net alone, but by the knowledge that it was there.

Looking through the small center hole up to the branches of the hemlock towering above him, Guillaume felt the same quiet pervading his being that he had felt on waking when he was with the tribe. Now, as then, his dreams had been good. They had been of a past to which he no longer belonged, but which had given him his songs; they had been of a cordelle that had drawn him into the present. He shifted his gaze away from the net and toward the old woman. Her eyes were on him and she was searching his face.

"How long?" he asked, first in French and then in the tribal talk he had used with his mother's people.

"Three days," she answered in French, holding up three fingers as she did so.

"It is so quiet." He tried to move under the weight of his covering.

"Yes, it is always quiet when men are away. They have gone to the post with their furs. They will return when the moon wanes. The girl and I are here to await them."

"And I?"

"You shall know all in good time. You are warm?"

"Too warm, and it is so heavy." Again he tried to shift his position under the animal skin.

"Wait." She laid her hands on him, then took away the buffalo skin and hung it on the branch of a nearby tree. She brought a lighter covering of deer hide, which she laid on him. Though the exchange had been brief, it was long enough for Guillaume to see his bare legs and thighs, blue as his shirt with the ugly spread of bruises. Almost with surprise, he saw that his hands were empty. The cordelle around which they had closed in the dream had felt so real.

"My head?" he asked, conscious of a slight pressure where there had been pain.

"It has healed, but I am keeping it damp for another day. It is better so."

"The girl, who is she?"

"Tais-toi! You ask too many questions. I have sent her to the lake for fish. This is the day I thought you would waken, and it is time now for you to have real food."

Guillaume moved his head. The certainty of food made him aware of hunger.

"You wish to eat, then?"

"Mais oui!"

For the first time during their conversation, Old Woman smiled. "Bien. You are getting well. You are young and strong. You will gain quickly."

Guillaume, though he could not as yet move his body,

lifted his right hand as if to take off his cap, and bow. "Guillaume Puissante, voyageur du Montréal, vous remercie."

"They call me Old Woman. I have been with these people many years but I am as you—half one, half the other."

"And the girl, she is your daughter?"

"No, Willow Wand is the daughter of the chief. Soon she will belong to Swift Arrow, one of the braves who brought you here. Let me help you sit against the tree."

She slipped her arms under him. Old as she was, she was stronger then than Guillaume, for it was more by her lifting and easing him into position than by any aid from him that she got him up and half out of the spruce bed to rest against the tree trunk.

Guillaume closed his eyes, steadying himself after the effort and against the throbbing it had aroused in his head. He smiled faintly. "I am weak, weak as a newborn limpet."

"But there is nothing to fear now, either for me or for you, Guillaume Puissante. Your strength is returning; like the sun when it comes into the morning sky, nothing can stand in its way."

She told him then what had happened—from the time his cap had been picked up on the water to the time the braves had brought him to the encampment and he had been placed in her care. After the telling, she left him to put wood on the ashes in the pit and move an iron kettle into the warmth. When she returned she had his sash in her hand. She helped him tie it around his waist.

"Moi, je suis voyageur!" The pride of his profession was again in his words.

She smiled at him, pleased with every indication, no

matter how small, of his desire for life. She handed him his knife in its fur sheath, his cap, and his tobacco pouch. He took them all gratefully and laid them on the duff beside him. They were his possessions, the marks of his trade.

"No pipe, no paddle," he said.

"The pipe must have been broken by the pounding waters that all but broke your body. There was no sign of a paddle."

"And my sac-à-feu is empty." He held up the beaded pouch, dangling it before him.

"When the men return they will have much tobacco with them, and it can be filled, if"—her voice took on a different tone—"if you are still here."

Guillaume sensed in her tone the warning felt by wild creatures when a jaybird flapped through the woods and called to them. He made no reply. For him to stay on, once he was strong and able, would be to become one of them, to live again the life he had known as a child.

She left him and busied herself by the fire pit.

"Old Woman," he called to her, and laughter ran with his words, "you who can make hurt ones whole, can you make curly hair straight?"

She did not answer.

Soon they had both directed their gaze toward the girl as she came up the trail from the lake and approached the clearing. She placed a string of fish on a flat stone near the fire and exchanged words with Old Woman; then she looked toward the spruce bed.

"You have come back to us!" she exclaimed, running to kneel beside Guillaume. "It was a long journey you went on." She spoke in the Chippewa tongue, and Guillaume answered her in kind.

"A very long journey—all the way from my childhood to now."

While Old Woman cleaned and prepared the fish, Guillaume and Willow Wand chattered together. She told him more about his rescue, and he told her what he remembered of the disaster. Much had gone from him and could never be recalled; much was unknown; but his struggle to retrieve his paddle was as clear in his mind as if it had happened a moment ago, as was his struggle to swim against the current with the rocks of the riverbed churning around him.

A smile flashed light across his face. "In the tribe they called me Brother-of-the-Beaver," he told her, pride in his words.

"You are Chippewa?"

He arched his brows. "Is the water of the lake not made of many lakes? So it is with the blood in a man's veins."

"I shall call you Brother-of-the-Beaver."

"Bien."

She puckered her brows at the word that had no meaning for her.

Guillaume laughed at her perplexity. It was all he could do to keep from lifting his hand and placing it on the furrows to dispel them. She was leaning so close to him that he could easily have drawn her face to his and laid his lips on hers. He spoke again in the tongue they shared, and trusted that his eyes, as they rested on her face and followed her moves, would speak the language no tongue could enunciate.

Old Woman brought a fish that she had broiled. Guillaume took it from her, and soon nothing remained but a small pile of bones on the duff beside him.

"You eat like a cat," she said in French, "clean to the last."

The girl looked from one to the other, for there was something they shared to which she was a stranger.

"Ah," and Old Woman nodded as memory stirred within her, "Willow Wand has never known the streets of Montréal."

"Tant mieux," Guillaume replied as he licked his fingers. "So much the better."

Old Woman brought him another small fish on a stick, and Guillaume ate more slowly while she and the girl had their meal. When they had all finished and the bones had been tossed into the ashpit, Old Woman helped Guillaume to slide down into the spruce boughs.

"You will rest now," she said. "Willow Wand will stay near."

Guillaume could do nothing but obey.

They watched Old Woman move off into the forest.

"You are better," Willow Wand said.

"Here I am strong." Guillaume laid his hand across his chest. "By tomorrow, perhaps, the strength will move into my legs and my arms."

"Old Woman has gone to search out more medicine for you. She finds it in the earth and in the trees, but she tells no one what it is she finds or where it lies hidden."

"That is her right."

"Your dreams were good," Willow Wand said, glancing up at the net.

"Yes." Guillaume wanted to tell her of all that he had experienced, but there was so much that she would not understand and that he could not easily explain. "It was of my songs that I dreamed," he said, "how I learned them, how I sang them."

"If you tell your dreams to me, they will be both yours and mine."

"I can only sing my songs, and only in French."

She settled herself comfortably beside him. "I will listen."

Pleased that she wanted to hear his songs, Guillaume hummed the tune of *L'Hirondelle;* then, drawing in what breath he could in his reclining position, he commenced. His singing was little stronger than his humming, but the words were clear and his memory could be relied upon. One song lent itself to another, and with each his voice gained more of its native power.

She listened while he sang to her of love in the lighthearted way of the jongleur, and to give him a breathing span now and then she chanted to him. Her voice was toneless and quite without rhythm, but Guillaume understood the words. He watched her eyes, thinking to see in them more than her lips conveyed; but they were the eyes of a forest creature, dark, wary, guarding inner secrets. Occasionally she laid her fingers on his lips for silence, and once she placed her hand across his eyes and held it there until he found himself slipping into sleep.

Among the shadows cast by the trees as the sun lowered and found its way through the forest in long shafts of light, Old Woman came. She swung a pot over the fire and stirred in it what was good for the evening meal. As the sun set and twilight filtered through the clearing, Willow Wand tossed fragments of birchbark into the fire to give light. The sputtering sound of the burning bark and the rich fragrance that came from it woke Guillaume.

Dismayed, at first, to see that day had gone, he soon felt gratified. Moving his arms, stretching his legs, even turning his body under the deerskin, he began to feel in possession of himself again.

Old Woman brought the iron pot over to the spruce bed. This time she did not need to help Guillaume to sit up and lean back against the tree. Willow Wand joined them, and soon they were all dipping into the pot with their fingers and drawing out pieces of meat. Guillaume dipped most often, and it was always the largest pieces that seemed to come to his fingers.

"Comme un cochon!" Old Woman said, sucking in her breath to hide the smile that trembled over her lips. "But tomorrow you will be a man."

After they had eaten and Willow Wand had left them, Old Woman tended Guillaume, washing the wound on his head, giving him a potion to drink that was the result of her earlier searching in the forest. Before she left, she told him that after another day in her care he could do what he liked.

"Is the dream net in place?"

"Yes, Willow Wand has seen to that."

She disappeared into the darkness, leaving Guillaume with the feeling that she was not far away. The warmth within the ashpit made the air above it quiver slightly; the fragrance from the bark still lingered. A loon called, and another answered. Guillaume knew from the direction of the sound where the lake lay and how far it might be from the clearing. An owl called, and another answered. Guillaume guessed that the forest behind him was deep.

Through the trees he could see the crescent of the

waxing new moon, perhaps two days old. As it lowered, the color deepened; nearing the horizon it seemed to catch a hue the setting sun had left. It looked like a little golden canoe sailing away from the night in pursuit of the sun.

The next day passed much like the first except that when it came time for the evening meal Guillaume sat beside the fire with Old Woman and Willow Wand. After they had eaten, he sang to them, and his voice sounded to him then almost strong enough to impel voyageurs on a day's march. Later, Old Woman removed the covering from the wound on his head. He explored the scar with his fingers.

Watching him, she said: "Your cap served you well. Without it, the stone might have cut deeper."

"Everything a voyageur has serves him well," Guillaume replied; then he wondered why he had said so. Without a paddle he was no voyageur, and he was not sure that he ever wanted to be one again.

Lying on his spruce bed, with the forest stillness broken only by its characteristic sounds, he watched the new moon through the trees. Holding between its two points the outline of its fullness, it showed what it would be when it made day of night. That time was distant. Guillaume counted the days on his fingers: all of ten, the way the moon looked now. It was not until the moon went from his sight that he recalled what Old Woman had said about the men's return. "When the moon wanes," she had said.

It was the dripping from the trees that woke him. Mist had gathered over the lake at night and rolled into the forest in silent gray waves. Caught by the trees, the moisture formed and fell in pattering drops. Guillaume opened his eyes. Only the merest break in the density of night gave him a hint of approaching day. Looking above him he could just distinguish the circular form of the dream net, see the moisture forming, gathering and running along the different threads toward the opening, then dropping through it. He opened his mouth and put out his tongue, curling it to catch the drops as they formed and fell. When he missed, they splashed on his nose and his chin. As the light advanced he became more skillful, and rarely missed.

The drops had no taste until he told himself that the width of the lake and the depth of the forest had met in the night and that this was their kiss. After that, the drops tasted honey-sweet, wine-rich.

As soon as he could discern the shapes of trees, he slid from under his covering, and stood up. Leaning against the hemlock, he saluted his legs as long-lost companions. Shifting his weight, moving his toes, he experimented to see if they would be obedient to him. He crossed his arms, then swung them to and fro slowly so as not to stir the air or intrude on the silence that was punctuated only by the drops of moisture forming and falling.

Sure that he was, at last, in full command of himself and that muscles and limbs would respond, he made his way silently down the path to the lake. Coming out of the forest to the broad expanse of open water, it was much lighter. Dawn could not be far off. In the trees nearby, birds were trying their voices as he had his limbs. It took little time to divest himself of shirt and sash, breechcloth and leggings, and glide into the water, swimming in the way of his childhood, so that scarcely a ripple was stirred.

Pushing himself downward, his hands felt the rounded stones on the lake bed. Coming up for air, he floated on the surface to rest and draw strength into himself; then he went down again and closed his hand around a stone. Treading water slowly, he rubbed the stone over his body wherever a feeling of uncleanness from many days' inactivity lingered. He looked back frequently to the shore where his garments lay, using them as a fixed point for return. The mist was lifting rapidly, and he knew that he could not now become lost in it. The water was kind to him, kinder than the land, for it supported him while it cleaned him and massaged him with its gentle motion. In it he began to feel as if he were being remade.

When he returned to the shore the sun had risen, and before its beams the mist totally dissolved. The day was gray no longer but golden, sparkling with light and new-ness. He took his shirt and washed it in the water until it, too, was fresh and clean. He held it from him like a banner so that the sun-filled air might start to dry it; then he put it on so that the warmth of his body could continue the drying. Now there was light enough to see his reflec-tion, for the water was almost as still as the mirror in the silver frame in Monsieur le Comte's room at the château.

Guillaume studied his reflection. With searching fingers he felt the scar that began at his temple and lost itself in his hair. His face was not to his liking, but remedy was within reach. Taking his knife from its sheath, he sharp-ened it on one of the stones from the lake; then he drew it carefully down the side of his right cheek, then down the side of his left, across the skin above his lips, around his chin. It was a long process, and during it the knife was whetted many times. Running his finger tips over his skin told him more of the result he wanted than did his frequent glances in the mirror of the lake. At last he was pleased. On this day of release into bodily power again, he would be an Indian, clean, smooth-skinned. He put on his clothes and tied his sash tight; then he left the lake and went back to the clearing.

The fragrance of the fire freshened by birch strips laid on the warm ash drew him quickly over the path, careless now of twigs snapping under his feet or the sounds made by dislodged stones.

The morning meal was in preparation, and at sight of him Old Woman gestured to the place where he might sit. The girl appeared and took her place. They ate silently, in respect for the food that broke the night's fast. Only when they had eaten and were full did they speak. Their talk was of the day. Old Woman had things to attend to that had nothing to do with the girl. Willow Wand had to procure food if they were to eat again. Guillaume had nothing to do but use his returning strength, so he accompanied the girl.

She knew an open place where berries were ripening, and to it they went. She led the way and he kept pace behind her. After an hour he was glad that she shortened her stride, for his was lagging, and when they reached their destination he was more than ready to stretch himself out on a sun-warmed slab of rock and lie still while she went about her gathering. The air was sweet with the fragrance of fruit, alive with the chatter of birds among the bushes.

Willow Wand picked until her basket was full. When she returned to sit beside Guillaume on the slab, he sang to her. The words meant nothing, but the sound pleased her.

"Shall I tell you what it is in your own tongue?"

She shook her head, and gestured toward one of the bushes. "I do not ask that bird to put his song into my tongue; why should I ask you?"

The sun was at the meridian, and they satisfied their hunger with berries. Willow Wand went off to refill the basket, while Guillaume lay flat on the slab, pressing his palms hard against its rough surface. With the warmth of the sun above and the warmth of the rock beneath, he felt he could never be cold again. Leaning on his elbow after a while, he watched the girl as she went about her gathering. What more could a man want than this? he asked himself. What more had life to give?

When they left the sunny clearing for the trail through the woods, Willow Wand stopped whenever she saw toadstools that she knew were good to eat, and picked them. Piercing each one with a porcupine quill taken from her tunic, she strung them on a leather thong that hung around her neck, then let the harvest lie loose over one shoulder. Sometimes Guillaume drew her attention to an especially bright one, of a red or yellow hue that put the sun to shame; but with most of them she shook her head and made the small swift sign of death.

The trail ran down to skirt the shore, and they neared the place where the stream flowed into the lake. Willow Wand laid her basket of berries on the pebbly beach; beside it she placed the string of toadstools. She ran swiftly toward the lake, over the pebbles and into the water until it met her thighs. She swam on the water, then under it. Surfacing, she lay in the lake's embrace until only her long hair lying on the water told where she was.

Guillaume was soon swimming beside her. He followed her lead, diving deep and swimming under when she did, meeting her face to face when they were both searching the bottom for stones. Because the distortion was so strange, and the impulse to laugh came over them both, they had to rise quickly in the wake of air bubbles that escaped them. They raced each other to the shore where a rock stood whose ascent she knew well. He followed her up it, followed her as she dived into the water, followed her when she splashed like an otter at play, followed her when she swam without rippling the water, and followed her at last to lie on the warm pebbles and let the sun dry them until her hair caught the wind again instead of resting lank on her shoulders.

"Brother-of-the-Beaver," she said, as if the name had been proved and could now be used.

"Willow Wand," he replied.

The sun was their guardian, and when it began to lower enough to cast a path of light over the lake, Guillaume tied his sash well and secured his knife to it, then challenged her to race him up the path to the encampment. Accepting his challenge, she wheeled and darted in among the trees; but he overtook her and reached the clearing before she did. Spent, but laughing, he threw himself down near Old Woman, who was stirring the pot in the ashpit. In a moment the girl had thrown herself down beside them both.

Again there was good food from the pot. Each took a share and ate in silence. After their meal, Guillaume sang while Willow Wand cared for the day's harvest and Old Woman busied her hands with watap, straightening the stringy fibers as if they were strands of yarn. Twilight was

long, and the moon had gained enough to give a notice-
able glow through the trees.

"It is not good to be near water without a canoe," Old
Woman said. "Today I have gathered what is needed.
Tomorrow you will start work on it until it is done."

"It will not be done soon," Willow Wand protested.

"There are many tomorrows," Old Woman replied,
"and this canoe is to be small."

As silent as a shadow, the girl left the circle of warmth
and went off to her sleeping place.

Old Woman stirred the ashes to make sure there was a
core of heat that would hold through the night. She spoke
to the fire, but Guillaume, listening, knew for whom the
words were meant.

"It may not be used, this canoe, but it is not good for a
voyageur to be without one."

"A canoe is of no use without a paddle, Old Woman."
She looked at him, closing her lips over words she would
not utter. Soon she left him, and Guillaume went to his
spruce bed under the dream net. The moon lighted something resting on the duff beside the boughs. It was a
slender piece of red cedarwood that widened at one end.
He closed his hands around it, and a surge of joy swept
through him as he held a paddle again. He felt like a bird
long deprived of flight who suddenly discovers it has
wings; then the surge was followed by another, equally
strong. He was no voyageur; he was one of a tribe. Soon
he would make the girl his, and he would be accepted by
her people. For three days he had sung of love and she had
listened; even though she had not understood the words,
he had faith that she knew what lay beneath them.

"Perhaps tomorrow—" he told himself.

"There are many tomorrows," Old Woman had said.

With both hands closed over the paddle, he had an almost uncontrollable desire to break it across his knee and put it among the embers of the pit. So doing, he would show Old Woman that he chose to remain. Then a loon called. In its weird laughter, he caught an echo of the mockery in the girl's laughter when she had led him in the chase. She was more aware than he of the difference between them. His hold on the paddle eased and he slid it under the spruce bed; then he lay back on the boughs and looked above him. He could see the moon through the dream net. It did not fill it. Many nights would have to pass before that could happen.

After their morning meal, Old Woman led the way to the place near the shore where she had gathered materials for the canoe. There were strips of white cedar for the frame, and for the covering birchbark that had been pulled from large trees in long sheets. There was a pile of watap to be used for sewing the sheets together. "When you are ready, I will bring resin for the seams," she said, and left them.

Guillaume stretched and shaped the cedar strips, calling on skills he had learned in his childhood and used more recently as a voyageur when nightly repairs were made on the canot de maître or the canot de nord. Willow Wand laid birchbark over the curved frame, sewing it firmly in place with watap. Guillaume sang often; sometimes Willow Wand fell into a chant. They said little; they laughed much. Several times during the day they dropped their work to swim in the lake and race among the forest trees in games of their own devising. Toward the end of the day, Old Woman appeared with a pot of resin that she had melted to the right consistency in the ashpit. Guillaume rubbed resin along seams that were ready to be sealed.

By the time the sun was dipping into the west on the third day, the canoe was finished. Because it was scarcely more than seven feet long, and correspondingly light, Guillaume portaged it easily to the shore of the lake. He set it down in a water depth of just over a foot. Willow Wand brought stones to be placed in the bottom of the canoe to hold it under water. Proud of their craftsmanship as they were, they knew that the last action would be that of the water as it caused the wood to swell.

"It is small, Old Woman; it will carry no more than two people," Guillaume said to her, "and we are three."

"If it carries one it will do its work," she replied.

He turned toward her and spoke rapidly: "Old Woman, I do not want to go. You have made me well. I have found more than a sister in Willow Wand. I will stay and be of the tribe."

She looked away from him and up at the sky. In the pale blue, the white oval of the moon could just be discerned. So like the sky in color, it was visible only to the searching eye. "The moon is not yet full," she said.

Usually the girl did not like it when they spoke to each other in the tongue they shared, but this time she did not seem to hear them. She had her own concerns as, with bits of bark and watap and strips of cedar left over from the making of the canoe, she fashioned an Indian village on the shore and filled it with small people.

Time was their companion, and it existed as if for them alone, as if they were the only ones within its scope; for Old Woman had somehow gone beyond time, and was impervious either to its demands or to its sequences. For

Guillaume and Willow Wand the sun rose to mark a day that was theirs, a day in which they followed shadow-flecked trails, swam in translucent water, and sunned themselves while he sang to her songs he had known before he knew their meaning; but now their meaning quivered in every note.

"What is this you sing of all the time?" Her lips stumbled over the pronunciation of *l'amour*.

"Ah—" It was the question he had been asked by the children of the tribe when he sang to them; the question he had asked of Monsieur le Comte. As he had smiled at the children and as Monsieur le Comte had smiled at him, he smiled at her, then sighed long and deeply. "Ah—hh."

That was no answer. There was wonderment in Willow Wand's face and furrows across her brow.

She leaned forward, and he bent toward her quickly to place a kiss on her forehead. She brought her right hand up to feel where his lips had rested, as if something remained. He seized her hand and ran his lips over the finger tips as if they were the stops of a musical instrument from which he might draw a melody.

The look of wonderment did not leave her face.

He sang to her, not in French but in her own tongue, a song that spoke of the delights of love; of the game that began with the eyes, then moved from finger tips to lips; of the feeling that rose in the heart and soon became the whole person. His words were delicate; his tune was gay— too much so, for still she did not grasp the meaning. "Do you understand now, my Willow Wand, m'amour?"

"Listen, Brother-of-the-Beaver, to what I say." In her low voice she chanted of the stream as it ran through the woods, of the lake as it lapped the shore, of the wind as it moved in the tall trees. The furrows left her brow, and the wonderment in her face lost itself in reverence, not for him but for the things of which she chanted. "Is this love too?" she asked.

"Perhaps."

She tried again, and told of the wild geese as they followed the pathway of the sky, of the otters as they played together, of the beavers. "Is this love too?"

"It may be."

She bowed her head, and her voice dropped so low that he had to lean near to catch her words. She told of the call a buck makes for a doe at the rutting season, of the fierce demand and the yielding compliance, then the drawing apart again. She lifted her head and faced him with her question. "Is this what you mean by your word, Brother-of-the-Beaver?"

"In a way, but there is another way, Willow Wand, that is tender, that grows like a small shoot in a green garden. In time it becomes strong. In all the world there is nothing stronger. When it is seen by two people for what it is, it lasts forever, and from it there is no drawing apart. Not on earth or in heaven."

Such transport seized him that he found no words for it in her tongue, and French words were of no use. He reached for her hands to kiss them, then held the palms against his heart; but she withdrew from him and kept her hands to herself.

"I know of only one way," she said. She bowed her head again, and this time her straight black hair fell forward like skins that close the entrance to a tepee.

He sensed her confusion, but it made him feel only more patient. In the silence that hung between them, he yearned toward her, longing to show her with his body what his words could not bring her to understand. Love as he knew it was as difficult for her to relate to her way of life as the French word was for her lips to shape. He could have seized her then as the buck the doe, so near they were, so remote in the forest, and she would have yielded; but something there was that came between him and his desire.

The medal of a saint worn around a man's neck could ward off danger; so did the talisman he carried in his memory. Monsieur le Comte's words rang through his mind: "Le seul péché c'est de trahir l'amour." To force her now would be to sin against love. He would wait. There were still tomorrows remaining. He took his knife from his sash, and idly fell to whittling on a piece of wood.

When she raised her head, she moved her long hair back of her shoulders, and smiled at him. It gave light to her face and broke the tension that had stretched between them. She leaped to her feet and laughed at him, merrily, mockingly. He stood quickly and tossed his head, ready to accept her challenge, whatever it might be. They were back again in the sheer delight of each other's company, racing like children through the green deeps of the forest.

During the long twilight when they sat by the ashpit, he told her of his saints. The evening was a gray one, and unusually still. Mist had rolled in earlier from the lake, and rain had started to fall, but under the tall hemlocks they felt it scarcely at all. Old Woman listened, as she did to songs or stories, and sometimes she prompted Guillaume to tell of a particular saint whose protection she had sought long ago before her life had been lived with a tribe.

Willow Wand had her own comment to make. "Brother-of-the-Beaver, all that you say is too far away. We pray to what is near, the sky and the earth. These great trees under which we sit are our saints. The summit of the nearest hill is our church. You say that a steeple bears a golden cross; I say that a brave standing tall is a steeple and that his uplifted hands can be crossed. You pray to people you have never seen. We pray to the sun and the moon, to water and clouds, and to the fleet creatures who live in the forest and are our relatives."

Guillaume shook his head slowly, finding it hard to understand her words, so foreign were they to his way.

Willow Wand fingered his ceinture fléchée whose gay colors lying on the duff between them captivated her. She gave a small pull to the two ends, but Guillaume had tied it too tightly to give to any touch but his.

Old Woman looked from one to the other, sucking in her breath to keep from smiling. "I have known both ways," she said, "and one will not bow to the other, but both will bow to an Unseen that nourishes the spirit as the earth we tread nourishes the body."

Guillaume began a story of Ste. Anne and of all she did for her voyageurs, but he ended by telling it only to Old Woman in French, as Willow Wand's lack of comprehension resulted in lack of interest.

"She will never understand. Her ways are different from yours."

"Give me time, Old Woman. Another few days and I shall *make* her understand."

Old Woman chuckled. Whatever it boded, she was

glad to see his self-assurance. It meant that her medicine had done its work.

As night came down, Guillaume left the warmth of the ashpit to sit alone by the lake in the cool caress of the rain and sing to himself a song of his own making that he would soon sing to Willow Wand.

Look forward as he dared, look back as he might, he knew that he had at last become a prisoner of the love he had long sung about. What life would be without her he could not guess; what life would be with her he was bold enough to face. It would mean being accepted as one of the tribe. It would mean facing Swift Arrow and asking him to come to terms. It would mean that their children would belong to the tribe. The mere thought that their love would so flourish made him giddy with longing to have her in his arms.

During the days that remained, time that was their companion was their guardian, too. The sun that rose for them alone set for them alone; the stars that shone from the great vault that arched over the lake twinkled only for them. But time was also their ruler. Guillaume knew, as did Willow Wand, that the moon had only a day or two left to wax. When it commenced to wane it would be, for Guillaume, as when a knell had struck; for Willow Wand as when the first snow falls through the forest.

Now, when he lay on his spruce bed, if he looked through the dream net at the time when the moon was high in the sky, the orb of the one all but contained the orb of the other. He felt his arms; they were strong. He felt his legs; they would carry him where he wanted to go. Only the scar on his head remained. It would be a reminder of another life, of a bitter experience that had proved to be the opening door to a time of bliss such as he had not known before. Reaching under the boughs, he felt for the paddle. He had more need of a bow and a quiver of arrows than of this, if he were to become one of the tribe and move back with them to their village from this temporary encampment.

One day, then another, and the moon was full.

A golden sunset lingered, and Guillaume stood by the lake, watching the glow as it faded in the west. Soon he became aware of another glow, less strong but persistent, in the east. The world of water and woodland would know little darkness on this night. He watched the moon rise. Its globe was pricked by the tops of pine trees; then, free of earth, it proclaimed itself an orb, round and perfect. He trembled at the sight as a man holding an hour glass might tremble, knowing that his life was running out with the sands. He breathed with relief when he saw that the orb was not perfect. But tomorrow it would be full. After that, it would wane. The moon was well above the trees now, and a slender, quivering path of light reached across the water toward him. It gained height rapidly. Soon he stood bathed in light.

Like a shadow moving through the forest, Willow Wand came to stand beside him. She laid her hand against his to tell him of her presence. He shook with joy, but silence was sacramental, and neither one spoke. He inclined his head to kiss her finger tips; then he turned and laid his lips lightly on her brow. Another moment and his lips would have met hers, for night had them in its arms.

She pushed him away with her merry, mocking laughter. "Day reaches into night, Brother-of-the-Beaver. Let us take the canoe and find their meeting place." Quick of movement, she darted from him and ran to where the canoe rested in the water.

He followed. Working together, they removed the stones that had weighted it, and drew it to shore, lifted and turned it to empty out the water, then righted it on the lake. She held the prow while he stood by the stern.

"There is no paddle."

Laughing again, she pointed to a tree near the shore against which a paddle leaned.

He went to get it. Closing his hands around it, he brought it with a swift gesture to his lips; then he returned to the canoe.

"I helped Old Woman make it on one of the days when you were so far away," Willow Wand said. "I knew where you kept it."

Guillaume's eyes widened. For a moment he was not certain whether he was pleased or dismayed to know that his secret had not been kept from her; but she looked so beautiful as she stood knee-deep in the water, with her hands on the little canoe and the white light of the moon around her, that he could only be pleased.

"Bien," he said, smiling.

They pushed the canoe out a little farther. She leaped lightly in to sit with her back against the curve of the prow; he climbed more carefully over the gunnel to kneel with the paddle poised above him. Delirious with delight at the feel of a canoe beneath him and a paddle in his hand, he sang lustily one of the gayest of the voyageurs' songs. As he came to the refrain,

> " 'Digue, dindaine,
> Digue dindé,' "

his blade touched the water, and the little craft shot forward.

When he came to the end of the song, they were near the center of the lake. He held the canoe still for a moment to watch for any seepage of water between the seams. There was none, though the whole canoe was still damp from its submersion in the lake.

"It is well made."

"Cedar and birchbark, watap and resin have gone into it."

He looked up into the sky at the jovial face that looked down at them; then he gazed at the girl sitting opposite him, and because she was just beyond his reach he flicked a few drops of water from the blade of the paddle toward her. She raised her hands as if to catch them, but she made no movement that would disturb the balance of the canoe. Into the path of light Guillaume paddled, and out of it onto the dark part of the lake; but the light kept drawing him. When the moon soared high enough, the whole lake became a sheet of light, and the path disappeared.

A beaver came out from shore and swam around them in a wide circle, lifting his head as if to see what new kind of animal had come to his lake.

"He knows you are his brother," Willow Wand said, quietly, so as not to disturb the creature whose lake it was.

A loon called.

She knows what it is saying, Guillaume thought. To me it is only strange laughter.

Silence enfolded them, broken only by the slapping of little waves against the canoe as it rocked at rest. He laid his paddle along the gunnel, scooped a palmful of water from the lake up to his lips, and drank. He began to hum

the tune of *L'Hirondelle,* but when he put words to it they
were the ones he had made himself to sing to her. In her
tongue, and as simply as he had told a story to the
children of the tribe with whom he had grown up, he
related the tale of the crane who, once he had found his
mate, never sought another; and when death came to her
before it came to him he lived on alone, content to remember their years together. His heart was in his voice;
his hands reached toward her, but she was just beyond
them.

When he came to the end she said, "You do not sing
of love tonight."

"I sing of nothing else, but I did not use the word, for
it is one you do not understand. Oh, my Willow Wand—"
He held his hands toward her, palms up and open, and
told her that the love he felt for her was a love like that of
the crane for its mate. As he spoke, the little craft moved
gently in the current of the water down the lake. "Now do
you understand how I feel about you?"

Again silence enfolded them. Her hands were in the
water, and by their movement she was giving the canoe its
direction around a point of land and toward a small sandy
beach that gleamed like a silver fleece in the moonlight.

"It is not true what you say, Brother-of-the-Beaver.
Birds may mate for a time, but not for life. It is not their
way. Never has it been their way."

"We make our ways, Willow Wand, and we follow our
hearts when we do so. My heart is yours and will ever be."

She shook her head, not in sorrow but with realism.
"When Swift Arrow wants me, he will take me, and I
shall be his for as long as he wants me. Brother-of-the-

Beaver, use your paddle and bring the canoe in to the shore. Tonight you may take me."

For a moment Guillaume could not speak, his voice was trembling so. "Willow Wand, it is not for tonight only that I would have you. I am like the crane in the story. I would have you for my mate for as long as we both shall live." He reached as far as he could toward her across the bottom of the canoe; still she made no move to bring her hands out of the water.

"You are not a bird; you are a man."

"Yes, I am a man." It was the proud boast of the voyageur, but he had done no more than whisper it. "Willow Wand, if you were to become mine—"

"You and Swift Arrow could both take me when you wanted me."

"*No!*" He brought the flat blade of the paddle down on the water with the force of a beaver's tail. The canoe rocked crazily. Guillaume, his pride stung to the quick, was deprived of words.

She lifted one hand out of the water and pointed toward the forest that rose back of the small beach. A tree towered above all the other near trees. Lean as a pole, it had been stripped of its branches except for a tuft near the top.

"We of the forest do not like what you Frenchmen do to our tallest trees."

His pride was stung again. This time it was not personal but professional, and he did not lack words when it came to defending the practice of lobbing trees. As he spoke, he began to back-paddle away from the shore they had been approaching. "Were it not for those lobsticks, we voyageurs would have no direction marks," he concluded.

"Brother-of-the-Beaver"—she leaned toward him—"let

us ride the canoe up onto the sandy shore and climb that tall tree. We might grasp the moon in our hands and bring it down from the sky as our plaything."

"No," he said. Paddling with short strokes, he turned the canoe and directed it toward the center of the lake, toward the pebbly shore where the stream ran into the broad expanse of water.

"Sing to me," she said.

So he sang to her of the love she could not understand and of which she would never know; she listened, for she liked the sound of his voice as she liked the thrumming of wind in the trees or the whispering of water along the shore.

When they reached the pebbly beach, she leaped from the canoe and waited while he brought it in, turned it on its side, and hung his paddle through the branches of a tree.

Her fingers were on his sash. "I would have you give me this," she said.

He shook his head, weary with the wisdom a few short hours had brought him. "Willow Wand, a voyageur does not part with his sash."

She searched his eyes with hers as she stood beside him. Never had she seemed lovelier than she did then. He could have put his arms around her and held her a willing prisoner, but desire had left him.

"Go now," he said.

"You will race with me?"

"Not tonight."

Accustomed to obeying, she turned and ran over the path to the encampment.

In a little while he followed. The moonlight sparkled

on the stream, speckled the path with shifting shadows. He walked slowly. After the fullness of light on the lake, the forest seemed dark and uncertain. He was not sure of his way. Old Woman was stirring the embers when he reached the ashpit. Willow Wand was sitting near. The warmth was welcome.

"Sing the song of the crane," she said to him.

Guillaume shook his head.

"It is good," she insisted. "I want Old Woman to hear it."

"The words have gone from me."

Old Woman went on stirring until a few flames leaped from the embers. In French she said: "But song has not gone from you, Guillaume Puissante. Sing what you will. It is the time."

He sang the song of the voyageurs when they moved into the river from Lachine—away from comfort and safety and womenkind into a land of waters and forests and dangers—*En Roulant Ma Boule.* He had not sung as a voyageur for a long time; his singing had been that of a troubadour. As the remembered rhythm came back to him, a different strength began to flow through his veins. When he reached the end, he began at the beginning again, increasing the tempo as if his canoe were approaching a rapids and the men must accelerate their strokes.

Sometime during the singing Willow Wand slipped away to her shelter, moving like a shadow among the trees. Old Woman did not shift her position, but with her fingers she kept the time, and Guillaume knew that she was French enough to catch the beat if he lost it. He ended with a flourish and a shout, feeling more of a man for the singing.

"You do not forget, Guillaume."

He shook his head.

"There is a time for everything."

He nodded.

"And for some things there is no time."

Their eyes met. They understood each other. She was old and he was young, but each one knew what it meant to be part Indian, part French. The double richness exacted a price.

"It is better so," she said. There was tenderness in her voice, as if she wanted to make amends to him in some way.

"Merci, je vous sais gré. You are right, Old Woman."

"Tie your sash well tonight, Guillaume, or you may not have it when morning comes."

His hands rested on it. His fingers explored the knot that only a voyageur could undo. "It is safe."

"But I think morning will not find you in the forest."

"You know so much, Old Woman."

"Ah," she said, and the sound was long-drawn-out and low, "of what use to live unless one learns what the years would teach?"

"Tell me"—hurt him as it did, he knew that he must ask the question that tormented him—"does she love Swift Arrow?"

"She will bear him children."

There was nothing more to be said. After a few moments Guillaume took Old Woman's hand in his and brought it to his lips.

"We do not meet again, Guillaume."

"I know that, Old Woman. Mille fois merci for what

you have given me—my life, and a paddle for le petit canot."

"And the dream net, Guillaume, that you must carry with you until you find the one of whom you dream."

"You think that I shall?"

"I do not think. I know."

He kissed her again, not on the back of her hand, but first on one withered brown cheek, then on the other. He went to the spruce bed with a light step. Before he lay down on it, he did what he had not done all the time he had been in the forest. He knelt on the duff beside the boughs and prayed to Ste. Anne. He asked her forgiveness that he had forgotten her for so long. Her feast, the twenty-sixth day of July, was approaching. Busy receiving praise as she would be, he knew that a single plea might fail to reach her; even so, he put himself in her care.

"Blessed Ste. Anne, remember me, your humble voyageur, Guillaume Puissante, who needs your protection." He prayed also to the Blessed Virgin, out of politeness, and to her Son, out of respect, but it was Ste. Anne whose help was sought.

Thinking of Ste. Anne recalled the immediate past to him, and he tried to determine how much time had elapsed since he had been away from his companions. It was the first day of July that the brigade had reached Grand Portage; it was a week later when the north canoes had set out from Pigeon River. Three days later, as nearly as he could remember, he had lost his paddle. Between that and the time when he had first seen the new moon through the trees, he could not say how many days had passed; but after the crescent there would have been fifteen to the orb. He who had always prided himself that he could not be lost in the forest found himself lost in time. Counting the days of which he was sure, he drummed them out on his chest.

"Sacré bleu!" he exclaimed, "but it must be long past Ste. Anne's Feast Day. It is St. Joachim's that is at hand." Fervently he prayed to the husband of Ste. Anne to intercede for him.

Relieved that he had put himself in capable hands, he flattened himself out on the spruce bed for what he knew was the last time, and looked up through the dream net. Soon the moon in its course would be in a position to fill the net, and for that moment he waited. He thought of the talisman of words that Monsieur le Comte had given him so long ago; he thought of the assurance Old Woman had recently given him. He prayed with all his powers that he would have the strength to wait for the one to whom he could give his love and who would return it in kind.

Now the moon filled the dream net. As if made to hold it, the slim circlet of ash wood encompassed the golden orb. Only light came through the interlaced threads and the small opening.

Guillaume gathered his few possessions together— empty tobacco pouch and sheathed knife. He slipped his feet, which had gone bare during the past days, into his moccasins. His red cap he did not pull down over his ears, but left it where the dream net had hung. This he now attached securely to his sash. She who had coveted a sash might scorn a cap, but there it was. If it remained on the branch, the weather would have its way with it; birds would pluck threads from it. But he hoped that Willow Wand would take it as his gesture and that it would hold for her some kinship to what the dream net would ever hold for him.

"Jamais." He whispered the word to the night, well knowing that it did not exist in her tongue.

Standing equipped and ready to leave, he was loath to go. Of all that had happened during the time of his sickness and his wholeness, he recalled the kiss that had been given him and that had drawn him from the twin torment of suffering and shame into a strange bliss, first in his dream, later in his waking. Because of that kiss he had been so sure that Willow Wand spoke a language they both understood that he had taken time to show her, through the little ways that were a Frenchman's art, what love might be for them. Living again that night and the exquisiteness of the moment when he had felt her lips on his cheekbone, he laid his hand against his face as if the seal of love might still be there.

Perhaps it was not too late to waken her, to recall it all to her, to speak more rudely to her in the way she understood. They would go down to the pebbly beach and push off in the canoe together, on to the white light of the lake, into the white light of day. They would find the brigade, and somehow a place for her would be found among them. She could not weigh much more than one of the pièces, and to make room for her a bundle of furs could be lashed in the small canoe to be cordelled in the wake of the larger one. It had been done before. In the stories voyageurs told around the fires at night, there had been many such. Then he shuddered, for the stories had had grim endings. There had been drownings; there had been runnings-away; there had been rivalries. Harshest of all had been the Indian uprisings and the vengeance taken on many for the folly of one.

The shudder dashed his imagining, and in a sudden new light he asked himself how he could be so sure that the kiss that had awakened him had not been given by Old Woman. It might have been the tender kiss of age, not the tentative kiss of youth. No, he must follow his course alone until he met the brigade. He had dreamed long enough. His heart might be heavy, but at least it was his own.

The path to the beach was familiar to his feet, and the woods were filled with light from the nearly full moon. By the shore, with the little waves playfully kissing its prow, was the upturned canoe. Guillaume reached into the tree for the paddle; then he put it to his lips, sure of its return of his love. The canoe was so small and light that he flipped it over with one hand and would have thrust it immediately into the water but for the sound heard from within it that he stopped to investigate. It was the sound of something heavy and loose, tumbling in the stern. He reached in, expecting to remove a stone, while wondering how it could have got there.

But it was not a stone. It was a square of pemmican tied with a leather thong. He stared at it; then he knew what it meant. It was Old Woman's way of saying good-bye.

"Oh, you are wise!" He tied it with its thong so that it would be secure under the upward curve at the stern. There it would be safe if he overturned. He gave the canoe a strong thrust into the water, waded beside it, and then leaped in to crouch, paddle in hand, in the long-familiar position.

The lake was a sheet of shimmering light. He pointed the prow toward the far western end, thinking to climb the lob tree when it was day and take stock of his surroundings. Exhilaration seized him at the freedom he felt. As he had not been made a casualty of disaster, so he was not to be of love. Were Willow Wand to ask him now what love was, he could answer her.

"It is what we two will never have," he would say. "It is to share joy; it is, at high times, to be of one body, but at all times to be of one mind and one spirit. You and I are what our lives have made us, and we are two. Love, if it is true, is something that will endure between a woman and a man."

Why had he said that? During his growing-up years in Montréal, it had not been so with Monsieur le Comte and his mother; and at the château he had seen much that went under the name but was not love. Willow Wand was not there to ask, and without a question there was no answer.

"Allons, we go forward," he said aloud in the silence of the moon-washed night. With his words he put the past behind him and accepted the future. What was ahead he knew no more than he knew what was in the next lake. When he reached it, by paddle or portage, he would see for himself, and that would be soon enough. "Moi, je suis un voyageur! Moi, je suis un homme!"

Chapter Nine

A CHILL WIND blew down the lake and rocked the canoe so that he stopped paddling to hold the craft steady. The wind was a presage of dawn, though day was still distant by several hours. The wind, on this late-summer night, was also a presage of another season. Winter was distant by several weeks, but it was drawing nearer with every passing day. One more moon would pass, and another; then it would be the Cold Moon, and white silence would lie over the land. Guillaume shivered, wishing he had his capote to wrap himself in. If winter imprisoned him before he joined the brigade or got down alone to Grand Portage, there would be no escape.

So much of his early life with the tribe had been brought back to him during the time of the moon's waxing that memory was easily stirred. Now, under the wind's cold thrust, he recalled the year when winter had come early and swiftly, too swiftly for his mother to get back to the château. They had been compelled to remain with the tribe. The braves went off frequently to hunt for food, while the women and children huddled in the lodges like animals in their burrows. But without the animals' benison of sleep, they were constantly aware of the body's demands—for warmth, for food to stave off the sleep from which none would waken.

The lakes were locked under three feet and more of ice; the land under six feet and more of snow. Pine and spruce and hemlock looked black against so much white, and the birch trees were the ghosts of warriors gone long ago to a land where the sun never grew cold. Those who cowered in the lodges forgot how to talk to each other, and when the braves returned they, too, were silent. Only the howling of the wolves echoed through the air, relentlessly, mournfully, for they were hungry.

Winter had been as slow to yield as it had been swift to come. When the snow had melted away and the ice had rotted on the lakes and finally sunk, the tribe reckoned a third of its people had been lost to the white death. His mother had returned to the city, then, and he had trudged beside her; but the journey had taken longer than usual, for they were weak and it was hard to find food along the way. How old had he been? Four, perhaps. It was the first year he had walked; other years he had been bound to the board on her back.

"Saccajé chien!" he exclaimed and started to paddle vigorously. If he was a man, he must act like one, and to idle on the water in the past was to be neither a man nor a voyageur. Should the trap of winter be in wait for him, he must be wary enough to escape it. The canoe moved forward to round the curving point of land from which the lob tree rose; then Guillaume pointed the prow in to the shore.

By the time he had beached the canoe, eaten a small amount of pemmican, and washed it down with water, the moon was on its way toward setting. Only a path of light reached over the lake. The remaining water was dark, restless with motion from the fitful wind. Guillaume estimated that there might be an hour to dawn, and another hour before daylight filled the sky. Until then it would be no use to climb the lob tree.

"Sleep when you can; eat when there's food," he reminded himself, and overturned the canoe to provide shelter. Taking off his sash, he tied it around the paddle and secured his two most precious possessions to the canoe; the dream net he tucked in beside the pemmican for safety. He stretched out on the sand under the canoe, and within moments was asleep.

Out of the surrounding silence a certain few sounds could be heard—the movement of wind across the water and into the trees; the flutter of waves on the sand; the sniffing of a mink inspecting the strange object that had come to its territory; the slap of a beaver's tail as it dived; the long calling of a loon; and, distant by the length of the lake, the roar of the rapids as water tumbled through the narrow channel and over the rocks to become the moving current in a larger body of water.

Only when the light began to change from black to gray to silver did the sounds change. A bird called like a trumpeter, and soon after the forest resounded with chatter and song. A pine squirrel with white-rimmed eyes and a black stripe over his back hurried down the lob tree and, at sight of the object on the beach, chirred warily, stamped his feet, and turned to race back up the tree. Dawn spread across the eastern sky. A rainbow of color widened, deepened, tinged the lake, then lost itself in day.

The sun was well on its journey when Guillaume awoke. So accustomed had he become to the bough bed and the dream net over his head that when, on opening his eyes, he saw the curved roof of a canoe, he had to struggle to orient himself. Rolling out from under his shelter, he stared at the lake and the wide arc of sky, watched a heron feeding on the far shore, then looked up at the lob tree to anchor himself. Sure now of where he was and why, he divested himself of his clothes and ran into the water. Washing himself with handfuls of sand rubbed over his body, he swam again to free his skin of clinging grains. Once back on the shore, he felt his face, running his hands down his cheekbones, above his upper lip, under and around his chin, hopeful that he could soon begin to boast the pride of a Frenchman. His knife now would be used only as a good knife should: to skin and gut fish, to shred wood for a fire.

Leggings, breechcloth, and shirt were quickly donned, and his sash, loosed from the paddle, was tied tight about his waist. He drew canoe and paddle into the protection of near bushes and went about gathering some blueberries to break his fast. Tossing them into his mouth, he went toward the base of the lob tree. He studied the holds that had been notched by voyageurs; he studied the distance to the tufted top; then, with a fervent prayer to Ste. Anne to be with him in the air as she was with him on the water, he began to climb. It was slow work, for many of the holds could be found only by exploring fingers, held to with one hand while the other hand searched out the next and toes gave support. The higher he climbed and the narrower the trunk became, the easier was the ascent. When he reached the tuft of branches at the top, he availed himself of the stoutest one on which to sit and study the land below him.

He saw more lakes than he could count, their waters

glinting in the sunlight. Above him billowy clouds moved in a leisurely manner across the sky, casting huge shifting shadows on the water as they came between it and the sun. Some lakes were rippling gently, and their water was so clear that he could see far below the surface; other lakes were covered with water lilies, both yellow and white, blooming from their green surrounding pads. In one of these he watched a moose browsing, lowering its great head under the water and coming up bedecked with long succulent stems and some of the flowers. He had a fellow feeling for the moose; in all the wide expanse below him it was the only visible form of animate life. Many of the lakes were dotted with small islands; many had rocky shorelines; and there were some whose margins were lost in the waving stalks of the wild rice that grew along them. He could almost tell by that sight how far the season had advanced. The stalks stood tall. Not one had yet bowed under its weight of grain. There was a full month to harvest, he told himself as relief surged through him.

If he had missed the brigade, if all the canoes had already passed this point on their way out of the pays d'en haut, he should be able to paddle his own way down to Grand Portage in less than a month, and that should be well before the first frosts came to whiten the land. He would have no trouble in finding his way back, as every lake they had come through, every portage they had made, had been impressed on his mind. It would take longer for one man in a light canoe than for eight men in a heavily laden north canoe, but he would use every hour of the daylight and the only time lost would be that required to find food. There were fish for the catching in the lakes, berries and roots in abundance, and as a last resort the tripe de roche. Moss had little appeal, but it could nourish when all else failed. The pemmican he would use sparingly. It was enough to know that he had it.

In all the maze of lakes and islands with their connecting rivers and churning rapids that lay below him, his way was clear. Back, across the road he had traveled. As he looked into the north and the west, he knew that was a road he could not have traveled. There was no way of telling on what series of marches the brigade had gone, or his own canoe with the full-faced sun on its prow. Each had been destined for a distant outpost. Another season he would know, but for this one his knowledge stopped at the meeting of the waters and the one lake beyond.

Gazing down on the world below him, a delicious drowsiness began to steal over him. The warmth of the sun was drawing fragrance from balsam and spruce; the movement of the air was wafting it up to him. He untied his sash and looped it around the trunk of the tree, then back around his waist to keep him from falling should sleep overcome him. He sighed happily. It was good, when on the water, to be in a canoe; there was no better place in the air than the tufted top of a lob tree.

Many a voyageur had sat where he was sitting. Guillaume felt their companionship as he saw the marks they had left on the tree. With some, it was no more than a slash made with their knives; with others, it was a crudely wrought initial. The slashes that had been made recently still had resin oozing from them. The tree had healed itself from the slashes of other years. Each scar told of one man, and as Guillaume drew his finger down a *T* and through an *X* he felt with friends again. He found himself staring at a small line of *P*'s. The first one had almost disappeared into the bark; the last one, well healed and dry, must have been made the previous summer. He ran his fingers over them and into them one at a time, wondering why they seemed to have more meaning to him than the other initials.

"Holà!" he shouted suddenly, putting both hands on the row of *P*'s as in embrace to a friend. He was remembering something, something that had happened such a short time ago that it might have been yesterday.

They were in the canoe, all eight voyageurs, and they were approaching the end of the long narrow channel where the rapids lay and the lake beyond. Resting on their last pipe and idling before their work commenced again, Prosper had lifted his paddle and pointed it to a tree so far ahead of them that it was all but lost on their horizon. It was a lob tree, the marker for their road, and Prosper was saying ". . . I shall climb it and put my mark near the top. It will be the twelfth time for me."

But he had not done it yet! Guillaume said inwardly, while wanting to shout aloud his discovery. If he had carved his *P* at any time during the summer, the cut would have been light in color and its edges would have been sticky with resin. Guillaume's fingers traced the *P*'s quickly, eagerly. There were eleven of them, and who but Prosper could have carved them? There were many men whose names began with *P*—Pierre, Pascal, Paul—but there was only one Prosper. Guillaume, studying the *P*'s, was as sure that they had been made by his friend as he was that the sun that rose in the morning would set in the evening. Other canoes of the brigade might already have gone by the lobstick, but not their canoe, not the canoe with the full-faced sun on its prow. Guillaume would wait for them on the sandy shore at the base of the tree. It could not be for long. Tomorrow might even be the day.

He shaded his eyes with one hand and searched the chain of lakes that lay to the west and the north; but all he saw was the widening V left in the water by a muskrat. He was too far away to see the small dark head that cut through the water, only the wake it left. He watched a deer and her two fawns step out of the forest to stand hock-deep and drink. Then his eye was caught by a curious object in the third lake. It was not an animal, for its course was too wavering; but it seemed to lack the direction of a man-impelled craft. Safe in the knowledge that he was too high to be seen by any eye but a bird's and that his canoe and paddle were well hidden, he watched as the object approached, grew larger in the second lake, and proclaimed itself unmistakably in the lake below him.

It was the canoe of returning Indians. They neither sang nor chanted, and because the strokes of the two paddlers lacked unison, the craft pursued a zigzag course. By habit they negotiated the channels by which one lake led to another; fortunately, there were no rapids to be run. With several hours of light left in the day, Guillaume thought they would not come ashore once they had rounded the point, nor were they apt to look at the tufted tree. They had their own way of finding direction, and a lobstick was a Frenchman's.

As the canoe passed below him, Guillaume had a clear view of its occupants. The one who sat in the middle, slumped forward in sleep, must have been the chief. Of the two braves, Guillaume thought that the one in the bow must be Swift Arrow, for the one in the stern, who was doing most of the paddling, answered to the descriptive

name Tall-as-the-Pine. This was the first time that he had
seen the men who had saved his life. Remembering all
that Old Woman had told him, and what Willow Wand
had later added to the story, he looked down at them with
gratitude and pity, breathing a silent prayer to Ste. Anne
to take them in her charge for the rest of their journey. On
the bottom of the canoe reposed several bundles. Guillaume could discern an iron kettle, several pots, and some
objects that from his height could not be identified, as well
as some that were still wrapped in canvas. A wooden keg,
obviously empty, rolled from one side to the other with the
motion of the canoe, telling its own story.

Less than three weeks ago, the canoe had left the
encampment loaded with furs, the result of many months'
work not only by these three but also by others of the tribe
who had remained with their women and children in their
village far back on the edge of the forest. At one of the
trading posts the furs had been exchanged for useful commodities, some trinkets, and much high wine.

Guillaume watched the canoe come through the channel, round the point, and pass the sandy strip of shore.
Like a drunken man tottering over familiar ground that
somehow called to his sense of direction, the canoe moved
into and down the center of the lake, then began to veer
toward the shore. If the gods of the water and sky were
willing, the canoe and its three occupants would reach the
pebbly beach where the stream ran into the lake long before
sunset. Probably Old Woman would know what to do for
them; or at best she might leave them alone. Willow
Wand—Guillaume blessed himself and murmured a prayer
for the girl.

Watching the canoe until it disappeared from his sight,

he breathed a prayer for Old Woman. She had known well
what she was doing when she opened his eyes to face the
future and saw to it that he had a little canoe with which
to move into his future. It would not have been good for
any of them if Swift Arrow had returned and found him
still there and enamored of Willow Wand. Finally he
prayed to Ste. Anne on his own behalf. This was the
second sign he had had in one day that all the canoes of
the brigade had not gone by.

"Ste. Anne, you are good to your voyageur, far more so
than he deserves, but I shall light a candle at your shrine
when I return to Montréal, and it will say more than these
poor words of mine." Sitting high in the tree, with nothing above him but the sky, he felt uncommonly near the
good saint, and found converse with her easier than when
his feet were on the earth. "No, I shall light two candles,
Ste. Anne, for the two signs you have given me."

When the last vestige of the canoe had gone, the V of
its wake that widened from one shore to the other, he
untied his sash from the tree, tied it about his waist, and
made his way from branch to branch, from notched hold
to notched hold, down the trunk and to the sandy shore
where shelter, food, and freedom all belonged to him.

Three days he spent at the base of the lob tree. He lived
well, spearing fish and cooking them over a small fire
made in the sand and so protected that little smoke rose
from it. His sac-à-feu might be empty of tobacco, but it
still held his fire steel, which served him. He gathered
berries and ate them fresh or dried in the sun on his
upturned canoe. He swam and sunned himself dry; he
washed his clothes and renewed stitches with hair-thin
strands of watap threaded through a porcupine quill. He

made brief forays into the woodland and climbed the lob tree in the morning and again before the light changed in the late afternoon. He sang the merriest songs he knew to banish loneliness, and often, while singing, he held the dream net in his hands and looked through the small round opening as if it could reveal in a daydream what it had power to do with a night dream. Sitting on the shore in the deepening dusk and singing of a lovely maiden who sat under an orange tree in a garden and tossed a kiss to her lover when he plucked a fruit for her gave him the assurance that, somewhere, a lovely maiden was waiting for him. Though he could not give her oranges, he could give her a beaver skin from which she might make a fine winter hat, and in a place like Montréal that would mean more than all the oranges on a tree. Because no song he knew said exactly this, he put his own words to one of his oftsung tunes, and instead of the refrain "Ra raderida" he shouted gaily, "À ton chapeau!"

A beaver gnawing away at a birch tree some distance down the lake left his work to investigate the sounds that were coming from the sandy shore. Guillaume, seeing the sleek head swimming near, then raising itself inquiringly from the water, sang to his audience of one. Curious, the beaver swam nearer, then in a wide circle, always returning to lift his head and stare at Guillaume. When, finally, he dived deep to return to his neglected work, Guillaume took the slap of his tail as deserved applause.

Dusk dipped to darkness; one star after another appeared. The breeze stilled. The water of the lake became calm, with as many points of light on its surface as there were in the sky above. A deeper darkness came down, a more intense quiet. Guillaume stretched out on the sand, rolled over into the shelter of the canoe, and slept.

On the fourth morning, from his vantage point in the tufted top of the great tree, he thought that he saw something floating on the surface of the lake that was farthest to the northwest and almost the extent of his vision. It had not been there on any previous day and it was definitely moving. Watching it, he could not identify it as any kind of animal or bird, or even any flock of animals or covey of birds. Moving steadily forward, down the very center of the lake and in his direction, he saw it approach the shore, disappear in the woods, and an hour later reappear, following again a midlake course. Becoming more and more certain of what it was, he did not want to leave his perch until he was sure. When he heard the faint sound of singing coming from it, he knew. Light as the wind was that day, its direction was favorable and it carried the unmistakable sound. It was one of the canoes of the brigade, but which one he would not know until it came much nearer.

Straining his ears now more than his eyes, he finally was able to catch the tune. From his place atop the tree, he joined in the refrain as lustily as if he were in the canoe and had a paddle in his hand:

> " 'Cach' ton, tire, cach' ton bas,
> Cach' ton joli bas de laine,
> Car on le verra.' "

However loud he sang, he knew they could not hear him for at least another hour of strong paddling and two lakes still to cross. He scurried down the tree and got his paddle from its place under the canoe; then he fastened it to his sash and went back up the tree to his perch. Once there and secure, he tied his sash to the paddle blade and waited until the voyageurs had come near enough for him to see which canoe of the brigade it was. After that, he would attract their attention.

Nearer it came, out of the farthest lake that was shaped like a turtle, through the channel of smooth-flowing water into the round lake that was studded with islands. He could see the craft well now, though he could not yet distinguish the design on its prow. It was as heavily laden with furs as it had been with commodities on the journey in; the voyageurs were bent to their task, paddling in unison and singing as they paddled. The canoe moved steadily forward. Hidden by one of the islands for some moments, it made a directional turn when it came into the open again, and the sun caught its own likeness in vermilion on the birchbark prow.

Though Guillaume could not see their faces, he said their names—Martin, Henri, Prosper, Michel, Hyacinth, Hypolite, Nicolet. They were one man short. No one had been found to take his place, and where he should have been sitting were two pièces cordelled to each other and to the thwart. Prosper, with a long paddle like that of Martin's, was using it first on the right side of the canoe, then on the left. Now they were approaching the channel that connected the lake they had traversed with the next one, and all singing ceased as they negotiated the narrow water. Guillaume could not hear Martin's words, but he guessed what he might be saying, "Lentement, mes voyageurs, doucement."

His heart was almost too much in his throat for him to

speak, and his eyes had so misted that he lost sight of the canoe. He swallowed hard and rubbed his fists over his eyes, then waited for the moment when they would be near. Out of the channel and into smooth water again, the current was bearing them so they held their paddles above their shoulders and waited for the steersman's word to bear down. But it was not Martin who gave it. From the perch, two hundred feet above the lake, Guillaume could see better than Martin from his height of less than six feet above the water the most advantageous moment to resume paddling.

"Allons-y!" Guillaume shouted, waving the banner of his sash attached to the standard of his paddle.

Reacting to the command, paddles bore down and cut the water, but instead of moving forward the blades were turned to hold the canoe.

Guillaume saw the voyageurs look at one another as if to ask from whence the command had come, since it had not been given in Martin's familiar voice. He heard an excited rumble of sound as they demanded of each one who had done this.

"Pas moi! Pas moi! Not I! Not I!" they were saying, and as no one of them had uttered the command, Echo could not be held responsible, nor was this a place where water running between rock walls could give rise to echoes.

"C'est moi! Votre ami! Votre compagnon du voyage!" Guillaume shouted again.

Martin looked up first and saw the colored streamer waving from near the top of the lob tree. "Levez les yeux!" He raised his paddle in the direction of the sound.

It was Prosper who discovered the small figure holding the paddle. "Ma foi," he exclaimed, "c'est Guillaume!"

"Pour l'amour de Dieu!" one voyageur said after another as he looked up the long trunk of the tree to the tufted top.

On the ground, each one of them would have dropped to his knees; in a canoe each one blessed himself with his left hand, since the right was engaged. A babble of sound could be heard among them. Was he alive or dead? they asked one another. Were they really seeing their fellow voyageur or was it the sort of vision that tired eyes could produce, a mirage to taunt them as they entered the lake where they had lost their companion?

Once Guillaume knew that he had been seen and recognized, he tied his paddle over his shoulders and scrambled down the tree to wait for them on the sand as they rounded the point. From branch to branch, from notched hold to notched hold, as he had done so often during the past four days, he made his way, quickly as a squirrel, carefully as a voyageur.

The men in the canoe, looking up again to the treetop from which the sound of greeting had come, now saw nothing. Hesitant joy turned to sorrow. Sure that it had been a mirage, they murmured: "Il est mort. Il est avec le bon Dieu." They had grieved for him when the accident happened; grieving for him a second time made their loss seem even more acute.

Martin gave the word they were waiting for, "En avant, mais lentement, très lentement."

Slowly the canoe moved forward. Slowly they would go down the lake to the meeting of the waters, without singing, for no man had the heart to sing. But first they had to move around the point of land, slowly, because of the change in current. They were silent, puzzled by what they had seen. Often one man or two saw the same mirage; never had it happened before that a canoeful of men had all seen the same thing and the next moment had the sight taken from them. What could it mean? Some crossed themselves hastily; others could be heard murmuring prayers.

When the canoe rounded the point of land and the men looked toward the shore where they had camped on the journey in, they had to believe that what they had seen so short a time ago at the top of the lob tree was not an apparition, not a mirage, but very life itself. Standing where sand and water met, legs spread wide, arms held high, with his sash flowing from his paddle like the banner it was, stood Guillaume Puissante singing the song they all loved:

> " 'En roulant ma boule
> Qui roule,
> En roulant ma boule.' "

Brown of skin, tousled of hair, with buckskin leggings and tattered blue shirt, he looked much like any of them except that he wore no red cap.

"Guillaume! C'est toi! C'est toi!" Seven men as one they saluted him, raising their paddles high before they cut the water and joined him in singing

> " 'En roulant ma boule.' "

No command was needed from Martin to turn the canoe toward shore and beach it as quickly as possible, but even in their excitement they moved with deliberation and care. Every man was aware of the flimsiness of the craft and the value of its cargo. When the prow grated on the sand, paddles were raised from the water and Henri leaped out to place his hand on the bow and steady the canoe. One at a time, but so lightly and swiftly that the motion was a continuous flow of agile bodies, the men leaped out. Martin was last, and he stood in water up to his waist. Paddle in one hand, the other hand on the gunnel, each of the seven voyageurs aided in bringing the canoe in and onto the shore, giving it a light lift at the last so that its exterior would not be grazed. Once it was secure, and only then, did they leave their task, drop their paddles on the sand, and run toward Guillaume.

Prosper was the first to embrace his friend. Holding Guillaume in the tight clasp of his powerful arms, he kissed him on the right cheek, then on the left, while tears rained down his cheeks to be caught in his silky mustache.

Guillaume could do nothing but submit to them, for only as each voyageur embraced the lost comrade could he prove to himself that it was Guillaume Puissante, in the flesh, a working comrade again.

"We lost much time without you," Martin said; "now, mon chanteur, we shall move again like the wind over the water."

The voyageurs dropped to their knees on the sand in a circle around Guillaume, and Prosper offered a prayer to their protectress. "Blessed Ste. Anne, mother of our Holy Lady, thank you for giving Guillaume back to us again—" His voice was so shaken with emotion that he could say no more.

"Notre Père," the men murmured, then followed with the "Ave Maria," their voices blending with the lap of waves on the shore, the whisper of wind in the trees.

"Priez pour nous, pauvres pécheurs, maintenant et à l'heure de notre mort."

"Ainsi soit-il." Guillaume said the concluding words, as the prayer had been in his behalf. He leaned toward Prosper, and whispered, "Is this her day, mon ami?"

Prosper shook his head. "Her day has gone by, Guillaume; we are far into the month of August. Where have you been so long?"

Nothing would satisfy Hyacinth but that they have a feast then and there, even though it was midday and by a voyageur's rules they would no more have stopped to eat before sundown than they would have stopped paddling. But it was not every day that a man given up for lost was restored to his comrades, and such an event could only be honored by a feast.

A fire was soon made, the big kettle set in it, and men brought water from the lake while Hyacinth cut a square of pemmican into small pieces to make rubbaboo. The thick soup, because it was had rarely, always made a banquet of an ordinary meal. While it was seething in the kettle, Henri brought the cask of high wine from the canoe and gave each man his dram.

"What hangs like the limp ear of a dog from your ceinture fléchée?" Nicolet asked.

Guillaume clapped his hand over his beaded tobacco pouch. "It has been empty, save for my fire steel, since I was last with you, mes amis. But—" he shrugged his shoulders with the gesture each man could interpret as he wished—"as I had no pipe, what would I have done with tobacco?"

Exclamations from the profane to the piteous ran among

the men. To be without a pipe was to a voyageur to be without the counterpart of a paddle, making a man as helpless in rest as he would have been in action.

Hypolite rose to his feet from the sand. Growling imprecations under his breath, he went to the canoe, fetched out his small bundle of possibles, and rummaged in it until he found a pipe. Returning, he presented it to Guillaume.

"But it is yours!"

"Of course it is mine. Do you think I would give you Michel's?" Deliberately he took a pipe from his sash and thrust it between his teeth. "Why should I not have two pipes? I have two eyes. Two arms. Two legs. A man needs two of every good thing."

"Merci, merci bien," Guillaume said, bowing slightly.

The other men crowded around Guillaume, taking from their own pouches, which were beginning to get low, pinches of tobacco for his empty sac-à-feu.

After they had had their rubbaboo, they lay back on the sand, and smoked. Knowing that Martin would allow them no more than one pipe, for the sun had already passed the meridian, each inhalation was savored; each release of breath was relished. Guillaume told them what had happened to him and of how Old Woman who had nursed him back to health had also helped him to make a canoe. He did not speak of Willow Wand; and if anyone suspected there was more to the story, no one asked.

At the conclusion Henri shook his head. "I think it was our Lady who had you in her care; even Ste. Anne could not have done all that for you."

"Pauvre petit," Prosper said tenderly as his eyes traveled to the scar on Guillaume's brow.

Guillaume put his hand up quickly to cover it. "It is my shame," he said.

"It is your pride, Guillaume. Wear it as a soldier does a medal." Prosper looked up at the lob tree, the long trunk bare of branches and the tufted top. "I have work to do before we leave." Knocking his pipe free of ash in the sand, he thrust it into his sash, felt for his knife, and left the voyageurs at their rest. He did not return until he had put the twelfth *P* in the bark, following the row of *P*'s. Wiping the resin from his knife, he announced to them all, "Now, no one can say that Prosper Mercier did not come this way."

"Êtes-vous prêts?" Martin reminded. "Are you ready?"

The men went to the canoe. It had been decided that le petit canot would be loaded with the two pièces that had filled Guillaume's place beside Prosper. Held by a cordelle in the wake of the larger canoe, there was no reason to think that the small one would not travel well. They laughed as they loaded it and fastened the load. It was light, but it had been made with care, and the men offered remarks about its future usefulness.

"C'est un berceau pour l'ainée de Guillaume," Nicolet said.

This thought delighted the men, and they began laying bets as to who would have the first baby born after their return.

"It will be Guillaume," said Hypolite, solemn as a judge.

"Moi!" Guillaume exclaimed, feeling his face flush.

"Pourquoi pas?"

Looking from Hypolite to Hyacinth, from Prosper to

Michel, and the others standing near, Guillaume realized
that their love for him was matched by their faith in him.
He tossed his head gaily. "Mais certainement!" Then he
gave the voyageurs' word of acceptance for whatever came
their way, "Moi, je suis un homme."

With all hands on paddles and gunnels, the canoe was
lifted lightly and eased into the water. Its prow was turned
to face the lake. Henri first in the bow and the others after
him in their continuing glide of movement, they leaped in
and took their places. Prosper reached under the thwart
and brought out a small bundle that he handed to Guillaume.

"My possibles!" Guillaume said, though little was there
but his capote. Seeing it, he knew that he would have
something to wrap himself in at night against the cold.

"Now I do not need to give them to Monsieur Bénédict,
but to the one to whom they belong."

"Merci, mon ami." Guillaume put his lips to the small
bundle, then hastily tucked it under the thwart.

Paddles raised, they waited for Martin's words. "Mes
voyageurs, at the meeting of the waters we shall portage.
It is long, all of six poses; at the end we camp for the
night. En avant, et chantez!"

The canoe moved out toward the center of the lake,
then down it on a course that was sure and swift. Behind
it the little canoe bobbed bravely. Guillaume sang with zest,
with release from the pent-up feelings of the past weeks,
with the bravado of one who has outwitted death and
returned to his work, and with a passion new to many who
heard him but understandable to them all. *À la Fontaine*
was one of the best of the paddling songs. Its rhythm was
strong; its words were gay; and its last verse gave every

man the chance to think of his own love, and rest in the thought of her fidelity. The eleven verses told the story of a young girl who went to the well to get water, and fell in. Three cavaliers came riding by and asked what she would give them if they pulled her out. She refused to say until she was out, and then she slipped away from them. Her heart was what each one wanted, but she told them it was not hers to give:

> " 'C'est pour mon ami Jacques
> Qu'a d'la barbe au menton,' "

Guillaume sang, with his own particular delight infusing the words; then the voyageurs joined in the refrain:

> " 'Ziguezon cotillon rigaudon tourlouré
> La diguezon le cotillon rigaudon tourlouré;
> Foulez l'étoffe, gling gling gling,
> Leve en-haut haut haut,
> I-ya-la ha ha,
> Foulez l'étoffe, gligne ziguezon tourlouré gai gai!' "

Racing the sun down the sky for no reason other than that they enjoyed so intensely what they were doing, they reached the meeting of the waters.

Martin wagged his head at Guillaume as the men prepared for the portage. "We have made good time, very good time."

"Le bon Dieu likes a song, and favors those who sing well," Guillaume replied. "Now, put a load on my back, for my shoulders have been lonely too long."

They placed a ninety-pound pièce of furs on his shoulders and secured it to his harness.

"Pile on, pile on!" Guillaume commanded.

So they put another pièce on him and fastened it to the tumpline around his forehead, slapping him on his buttocks so that he might be on his way and out of theirs.

Straining into the line and starting forward, Guillaume gave a wave of his right hand in hasty thanks. After his month of inactivity, it was good to feel a weight on his back again, good to feel the sweat pour down his face and run cold as it trickled onto his bare chest. Bent almost double as he was, in his joy at being alive and free and with his comrades again he felt that he could have taken the weight of the world on his shoulders.

"Moi, je suis un homme," he told himself, treading carefully for all his proud boasting. The first few steps over the portage reminded him how precarious was the balance of the two pièces and how treacherous the stone-studded path could be.

Chapter Ten

THAT NIGHT, as they sat around the fire with sashes unloosed, the men told Guillaume the story of their voyaging—through smooth waters and rough, hot days with their clouds of insects, and days when a mizzling rain made their work as pleasant as a voyageur's could be this side of heaven. They told of the Indians who had come to the trading post with furs to barter for the tools they needed and comforts they enjoyed, and as they spoke Guillaume remembered that among the swarthy bargainers were the men who had saved him, Tall-as-the-Pine, Swift Arrow, and their chief.

"When all the bartering was done and the settlements made," Martin concluded, "we had a great feast. Everyone was happy. The Indians got the things of civilization that mean little to us, for we have always had them, and we got the prime pelts that mean nothing to the Indians, for there are always more animals in the forest."

"And everyone had too much high wine," Hyacinth added.

"But not until the last day when trade had been done."

Hyacinth shrugged his shoulders. "I did not say when it was, only that it was."

Hypolite puffed at his pipe and spoke through spirals of smoke. "No Frenchman ever had too much high wine."

"A Frenchman knows what to do with high wine," Hyacinth said; "for an Indian, even a little is too much."

"But, mon ami," Prosper added in his sage way, "if an Indian chooses to put a winter's work on his trapline into a night's drinking, is it different from what some of us may do when we get back to Montréal—spend our summer's wages on a night's fling?"

Heads nodded. A month ago they would not have let themselves talk this way, but now with their faces turned east they could begin to think of Montréal as if it existed; they could begin to tease themselves with thoughts of what waited for them at the end of their season's work.

One voyageur after another left the circle by the fire, sought out his place that he had reserved for sleep, rolled himself in his capote, and welcomed whatever dream might come to him. Soon only Prosper and Guillaume were left by the fire. Prosper, smoothing his fingers over his mustache, looked slyly at Guillaume. "You will be a Frenchman again one day if you give it time, but why did you work so hard to become a smooth-skinned Indian?"

"Ah—" The sound Guillaume made told the story.

"Was she beautiful?"

"As the dawn."

"And young?"

"A flower just opening."

"You could not make her yours?"

Guillaume shook his head.

Prosper sighed. Soft as the sound was, it had in it the long reach of sympathy. "I guessed as much, mon ami."

"How was it that you did?"

"By the way you sang today. That told me more of what the past time has been for you than any words of yours ever could."

"She could not be mine," Guillaume paused, then added, "ever."

"Or forever?"

The question required no answer, but Guillaume gave it, letting his head droop forward until his chin touched his chest, and saying almost inaudibly, "C'est vrai."

Prosper laid his hand on Guillaume's. "I am old, mon ami, more than twice your age, and I may not have many more voyages to make to the pays d'en haut, but this I say because I have not only loved but love: He who will not settle for second best but waits for the best will find it waiting for him."

Guillaume lifted his head and looked at Prosper. In his eyes were the words he could not say and the hope that what his friend said might be true.

"You have done well, mon grand. Love must be all or it is nothing."

Guillaume breathed deep and his chest swelled under his blue shirt. Only one person had ever before called him "mon grand." He smiled at Prosper. "Merci, mon ami."

Without further words, each left the fire, searched out his capote, and rolled himself in it close to the upturned canoe. Guillaume was glad to have the warmth of his capote around him again. The August nights were tinged with a chill the July nights had not had. Prosper stayed awake long enough to breathe a prayer for his friend and put him in the care of good St. Valentine, who understood the things of the heart.

Hyacinth woke them at three o'clock with his familiar call, "Alerte! Lève, lève, nos gens!"

Neither moon nor stars could be seen in the shrouded sky, but the flickering flames under the kettle gave what light was needed. The meal of dried peas and lard cooked to an edible mush was soon dispatched; the canoe was loaded, and they were off on their next march. Moving out from shore a few lengths, the canoe was held steady for a moment so Martin could make certain that the loading had been well done and the balance was right. At his command, they paddled slowly, feeling their way in the darkness to midlake, following Martin's directions. Guillaume gave the pitch of a song, then hummed the first verse through. Before starting his real singing he breathed deep, as if to breathe in the air of the mist-shrouded morning that he might give it out in song.

Soon the gay words and tune of *C'est Là Mon Doux Plaisir* sounded across the water, waking the birds who were still asleep in their forest haunts and advising the nocturnal creatures that though night had not entirely gone, day was at hand. It was a lively song, and the men sang it gleefully. They had a real feeling for the girl whose father thought she was too young to marry but who convinced him that she could boil soup, grill fowl, tidy up her happy home, "And make the bed at night." The refrain was no more than a ditty, and they sang it with gusto:

> " 'Je l'aime tant, mon ami,
>   C'est là mon doux plaisir.' "

When light covered the lake, Martin called for the first pipe. The canoe rested on the water as the men filled clay bowls from beaded pouches and smoked in silence. When Martin tapped on the water with his paddle, there was a last long-drawn breath on the all but empty pipes; then the stems were tucked into sashes, hands closed around paddles again, the voyageurs bent forward and waited for the words that would send them on their way, "En avant!"

They reached Pigeon River the day before the feast of St. Louis, August 25th, the last canoe of the brigade to come out of the pays d'en haut. They were late, and no one knew better than Martin what their lateness might mean, but he would explain it to the agent of La Compagnie Pelleterie. There would be no sorrow for him as he made his explanation, but joy, since the man they had given up for lost had been restored to them again. "C'est un miracle." And if they had been blessed by one miracle, why should they not expect the weather to help them back to Montréal in the brief two months remaining to them?

The canot de nord was emptied of its load of furs at Pigeon River, drawn well ashore, and left with the other north canoes that had served during the summer through the lakes and rivers of the pays d'en haut. Their supplies and equipment, and the many pièces of furs, would be portaged down the trail to the warehouse at Grand Portage. There the pièces would be unpacked, repacked again, and loaded into the big Montréal canoe for the journey back. The men had worked hard and well, harder than many of the other north canoes because they had been a man short during a good part of their way; they were entitled to several days' respite at Grand Portage, but Martin knew they could not spare the time. Once the big canoe was loaded and the six men rejoined them again to bring the paddlers up to fourteen, they would have to be off on the two-thousand-mile journey to Montréal.

"Allons, allons," Martin called to the men as, with their loads on their backs, they started down the trail.

Each man would have to make at least two trips, and Guillaume would make a third for the sake of le petit canot. "Voilà, nous marchons!" they shouted back as they bent to their loads, leaned into their tumplines, and started down the nine-mile portage, one behind the other. Without song, each man had to find the pace and rhythm that best suited him. Downhill as it was, they had no breath for singing but plenty for shouting imprecations at stones or for boasts of their own strength or supplications to a patron saint.

Near the end of the trail was a point where the forest rolled back and away on either side as if a great hand had pushed it, and through the opening their goal could be seen. Here a pose was always called; and, standing still and breathing hard, the men lifted their heads enough to see the cluster of buildings at the bottom of the hill where the blue flag of France was flying.

"Vive la France!" Prosper shouted, and, like one of their choruses, every man joined in repeating the words.

Beyond were the waters of the great lake, blue as the background of the flag or the firmament of heaven, shining in the sunlight. There was activity at the landing place as one of the long, heavily laden canoes was just leaving. Another, with its voyageurs in position and paddles raised above their heads, was waiting to leave. One upturned canoe remained on the shore. That was theirs, but they could not hope to be off in it for at least three days. From their vantage point at the top of Mount Rose they shouted to their fellows whom they would not see again until they met in Montréal.

"Bon voyage!"

"Au revoir!"

In spite of the loads on their backs, the men shouted until their voices were heard and one man in the waiting canoe turned and saw them. He raised his paddle in recognition and drew the attention of the others to the group on the hilltop. Paddles were raised, as were voices, and fitting salutation made for those who were soon to embark, for those who were arriving at the point for embarkation. Because of the loads on their backs, the voyageurs on Mount Rose could not drop to their knees, but each one could pray for his fellow voyageurs. Blessing themselves, they murmured their Notre Pères and added a special plea to Ste. Anne. Someone would do the same for them when it was their time to push off on the great lake.

When the first canoe was well out from shore, the second glided into the water, both of them heading for no visible horizon. Paddles dipped, voices were raised, and the long canoes that sat so low in the lake were on their way. The men on the hill cheered; then they strained their ears to hear the song that came faintly over the distance.

"It is *C'est l'Aviron Qui Nous Mène*," Guillaume shouted.

Eight voyageurs standing on the hill—red caps on all but one, feathers in all but two of the caps—sang with the twenty-eight voyageurs on the lake in their two canoes. It was the song that had not yet been sung, the song always saved to shorten the journey home with the promise of what lay before them, "the prettiest demoiselle." Led by Guillaume, they came in strong on the refrain:

" 'C'est l'aviron qui nous mèn', qui nous mont',
C'est l'aviron qui nous monte en haut.' "

Forgetful of the loads on their backs, they sang until their eyes could no longer see either the first canoe or the second on the water or their ears hold to the sound coming from the homeward-bound voyageurs. The pause and the participation it gave them with their fellows left them with new zest, and they plunged merrily down the rest of the steep path through the forest, under the great trees that arched over them like the vaulted roof of a church. The muffled tread of their moccasined feet was all that could be heard.

When the pièces were all delivered to the warehouse, Guillaume made his last trip alone and came down easily portaging le petit canot. Frequently during the past few days he had made certain that the dream net was safe in the place where he had tied it; the pemmican he had given to Hyacinth for the next time he chose to make rubbaboo. When he placed the small canoe on its side near the large Montréal one, he reached in under the curve of the stern and took out the dream net; then he wrapped it with his possibles in his capote and left the bundle under the thwart where he and Prosper would soon be sitting. He patted the small canoe tenderly. Ever since the men had called it a cradle for his first baby he had had a special feeling for it. The men had all gone off to the church to be shriven by the priest in preparation for taking communion on the next day, the feast of St. Louis, onetime King of France. Guillaume soon joined them.

Martin had no intention of asking the men to work on a feast day, but they were so used to activity and so eager to get home that as soon as they came from church that morning they started to load the canoe.

When afternoon shadows began to appear, Hyacinth reminded them, "Tonight the company will give us a banquet. We shall have more food than we need and more hours of rest than any of us can use. Tomorrow we shall be glad to be in the canoe again."

Soon after dawn on the twenty-seventh day of August the eight men, joined by their six companions of the outward journey, took their places in the canoe. More than two tons of furs made up the cargo, and the value was many times that of the commodities they had brought in to Grand Portage. They were the last canoe to leave, and the people of the tiny settlement came down to see them off as they had been on the shore to welcome them. Except for a stray adventurer, there would be no one from the cities on either side of the Atlantic Ocean until the first canoe came through at the end of June.

The warmth of the early morning foretold a hot day. A haze quivered over the water. The great lake was calm.

"May le bon Dieu and Ste. Anne protect you," said the priest as he made the sign of the cross over the canoe.

"And St. Michael, too," replied Martin, "for it is on his day that we shall hear the waters of the rapids at Lachine sounding in our ears." To himself he added, "If weather and winds are kind and all goes well."

"So long?" Guillaume queried Prosper. The day before the last day in September seemed then like an eternity away.

Prosper shook his head. "We will not return by then,

and no one knows it better than Martin. The journey in took us close to eight weeks; the journey out may be done in six, for the west wind will help us. Once we get to the great river we will not work against the current but be borne on it."

"We are harder now than when we set out last May," Nicolet added.

"But why does he say St. Michael's day?" Guillaume pressed.

Prosper stared at him. "Always we hope for the impossible! And, Guillaume, if you do not leave room in your day for the miracle, you are more Indian than I thought."

"À Dieu ne plaise!" Guillaume exclaimed, putting his hand up to his cheeks to feel the beard that was beginning to sprout. "Je suis Français."

"Bien," Prosper said proudly, "bien."

"If St. Michael has us in his charge," Guillaume added, "surely all the angels of heaven who do his bidding will come to our aid."

"Look!" Prosper pointed excitedly in a westerly direction across the lake. "The Old Woman is ruffling her skirts."

No more tangible blessing could be theirs than a wind at their backs as they started off. If it stayed steady, they might even be able to use the sail, thus adding hours as well as miles to their day; but if the Old Woman did more than ruffle her skirts they would have to paddle doubly hard and fast to keep from being blown upon the rocky shore, and their day would lose both hours and miles.

Left hands went into tobacco pouches that had been well filled by the agent of La Compagnie Pelleterie; fingers scattered pinches on the water. Pray to God but appease the Old Woman if you would cross the great lake safely was a rule known to every voyageur. Martin gave the word they were waiting for; Guillaume gave the pitch for the song. Paddles cut through the water; voices rang out strong and gay.

Chapter Eleven

TWO THOUSAND MILES of water lay before them: calm and turbulent, treacherous and safe. At the end was Montréal, the city of their dreams, its people those of their hearts. That was the vision before them now, and in it was the strength that powered them. As soon as one song was sung, Guillaume commenced another. The sound of their singing reverberated through the air as the wake of the big canoe with the tiny one chucking behind it rippled over the water. When the Old Woman ruffled her skirts a little too audaciously they sang *V'Là l'Bon Vent* to conciliate her. Whether it was the song or Martin's slight change of course, they lost no time that first day to her whimsies.

"We have as much breath as She has," Guillaume said as he led off in *Je Sais Bien Quelque Chose*.

The story of Marguerite who walked through the fields weeping because her father said she must marry an old man was a long-time favorite with the voyageurs. Each one saw himself as her savior. Old men might have money, but young men had wit. It was not enough to sing the refrain only. When Guillaume came to the words:

" 'What a good thing 'twould be if
All these old men were taken
Many miles out to sea to
Starve and die forsaken!
Let the old men have crones.
Maidens they should not tether.
Crabbed old age and youth
Never can live together.' "

the men sang too, bearing down on their paddles as if they would drown all the tiresome old men who made the Marguerites of the world weep. Then, with the feeling of a worthy task accomplished, they came into the refrain:

" 'Je sais bien quelque chose
Que je ne veux pas dire,
Ah!
Que je ne dirai pas.' "

Retracing a road they had traveled earlier in the season gave them the advantage of the familiar in many instances, though familiarity was never to be wholly trusted. Rocks could shift; water levels frequently changed; and for these, Henri's eyes from the bow and Martin's as he stood in the stern were always searching.

The pattern of their days had been established when they first set out from Montréal—marches interspersed with pipes, portages with poses, work-filled days, nights of deep sleep. One day varied from another only in the weather it brought, but weather made little difference to them. When it was good it aided them and gave them time; when it was bad they had to work harder, and it stole time. When a light rain threatened, they stripped to the bare skin, folded their clothes to sit on and so kept them dry. Rarely did rain hold them shorebound. If it was heavy enough to swamp a canoe, or if the wind turned up boisterous waves, they did not venture from their camp; nor did they if mists rolled over the water thick enough to muffle sound, for Martin needed to hear as well as see for sure direction. When they were shorebound, they rolled themselves in their capotes, found soft beds among the pièces under the canvas, and slept the time away.

Generally rain smoothed the water so the canoe skimmed over it speedily; and rain made the insects disappear, though midges and mosquitoes were not so prevalent in September as they had been in June. Rain, heavy or light, made portaging difficult. A man could carry only one pièce when the ground was slippery, and frequent trips had to be made. Rain was always the reminder to press on, press on, for the seasons were due to change in a few weeks, and the change could come sooner rather than later. Many a veteran voyageur had a story he could tell of someone, often himself, who had been caught by the weather and held prisoner in the pays d'en haut. He would not tell it, only hint darkly at it, while they were journeying; to tell it might bring on bad luck.

"Someday you shall hear the tale of pauvre André," Hypolite announced one evening as the voyageurs sat in the warm glow of their campfire. No one asked for more, nor did he offer another word. The voyageurs knew when that someday would be—on a winter night in Montréal when the wind piled the snow up against the windows, wood crackled in the stove, and wife and children were near and accounted for. Then Hypolite could safely tell the story of pauvre André, and if it grew in the telling there was no one who would dispute it.

The rain they blessed and cursed came often, but even in September the skies could hold rain only as a cask held wine, and when it was used up there was no more for a time. Through halcyon days with their calm waters and kindly suns they paddled and sang; through star-studded nights until the moon began to gain enough to provide a pathway of light. One such day followed another. At night, when Martin unfolded his map to mark their course, he rewarded the men with a dram of high wine if a hundred miles had been accounted for between morning start and evening rest.

"Ça fait bien," he said, smiling at the group of tired and hungry men crouched near the fire, eating their meal. "Tomorrow we will do the same. C'est pour la gloire de Ste. Anne."

They raised their drams in salutation to the saint in whose care they were.

If Martin had asked them then to reload the canoe and paddle through the night, they would have done it, grumbling, swearing, but willing. He did not ask them, though he knew he might have to if a storm threatened that would delay them. While they danced their rounds and sang, Martin walked back to the shore. Standing there alone and quiet, he studied the sky to determine the next day's weather from the shapes of the clouds and the wind's bent.

"Le temps fait beau," he decided, as he turned back to join the others.

Even during a succession of fine days they did not yield

to the temptation of thinking such weather would last forever. In their hearts they knew that it might break any day: wind could shift from the west to the east and instead of helping them could hold them almost at a standstill; such a wind could bring storm so their day's goal would become not a hundred miles but the nearest landing place.

In June and July, time had been so freely given them that they could squander it. Dawns broke early, dusk settled late; sometimes the dark between the two was negligible. Warmth enfolded them like the arms they sang about so exuberantly; clouds of gnats enfolded them, too, but these gave them a chance to exercise their vocabularies as they execrated them. Unable to slap at them with their hands because of the paddles, they hurled oaths at them that, though they had no effect on the gnats, tended to mitigate the annoyance of their stings. Between songs this gave good vocalizing, and invariably the man who could sing most endearingly could swear most convincingly. Time had been with them once, and they had used it freely; now time was as precious as the last liter in a cask of wine. As every drop would be savored, every moment would be valued.

They had made the portage of many poses at Sault-Sainte-Marie, and while near the trading post had filled their pouches with tobacco. Martin paid for it from company money, since tobacco was as necessary for their well-being as were dried peas and lard. The cask of high wine was replenished and set carefully in its place in the stern.

"Have you enough?" Hyacinth asked.

"Enough if all goes well," Martin replied, "and if it doesn't, no amount of high wine would do us any good."

"When shall we reach Montréal now?" Guillaume nudged Prosper.

"Martin hopes that it will be by the Feast of St. Luke, but he will not say."

"Why will he not say?"

"Because it must be by that time. The eighteenth of October is too close to the coming of winter for safe traveling beyond that day."

"So we must have no more bad weather to cause us to lose time?"

"Martin allows for some bad weather, but not much, not much." Prosper thrust his hand in the water and took it out quickly. "It is cold enough to freeze a man!"

"But not to form ice."

"No, but that will come. A man is not made of water, Dieu merci, but of blood, and oh, how soon that can freeze!"

Guillaume shivered, impatient for Martin's "En avant!" Just then it seemed that only singing with all the breath in his body could warm him against the oncoming cold.

They were in Lake Nipissing, and a long stretch without any portages lay before them. The men were in high spirits as every stroke, every mile put them nearer to Montréal. Now, when they were not singing of love they talked of it, boasting of their women, telling each other of their wives' prowess in childbearing and cooking, in spinning, weaving, or any of the many skills a woman knew. Each man was ready to defend the reputation of his own woman even to the extent of blows; but hands were needed on paddles, so the only blows that could be dealt were words.

"You waste your breath!" Martin shouted above the babbling voices. "Chantez, Guillaume."

So Guillaume, who had no woman of his own to defend but who could boast as well as any of them, led them into *Cette Aimable Tourterelle*. It was short, only three verses, and it had no refrain, so they sang with Guillaume, and both words and jaunty music complemented their high spirits. Forgetting for a time each one his own, each sang of the little brunette in Paris:

> " 'I know not if she's mine to be,
> This lovely turtledovey-dovie;
> This perfect little beauty.' "

Each knew she would be his, for soon he was singing what she was ever telling him:

> " ' "Oh, how happy we shall be,
> When we are married, you and me." ' "

By the third verse, each one had somehow left Paris and the little brunette far behind and was in Montréal with his own true love. Guillaume changed the tempo, making it slower, dropped the pitch, making it more sentimental, and the men sang tenderly of the promise each would give:

> " 'I give my hand to turtledove,
> She gives me a rose, a rose away.
> And turtledove she smiles to me:
> "Oh, be my lover faithfully!" ' "

Sensitive to their present mood, Guillaume led them in *Le Miracle du Nouveau-Né* with its gentle refrain:

> " 'Je suis jeune; j'entends les bois retentir;
> Je suis jeune et jolie.' "

It was a long, sad, tender song that could always be counted on to soothe spirits and take the edge off rivalries. By the time they had sung it three times, their thoughts had turned to their children and were quite away from their wives. They began to lay bets with each other as to whether the new inhabitant of the cradle would be a son to follow in his father's footsteps or a daughter to stay home and help her mother. There was no money with which to fund a bet, so one man cheerfully laid his ragged shirt against his fellow's faded cap, another a neckerchief against a capote; but no man bet his ceinture fléchée no matter how certain he might be.

Martin called through their talk to turn toward shore. The men grumbled but obeyed. The day was fine. There was much smooth water ahead. Why should they end their work so early?

"That you may begin again," Martin said, and they knew what he meant.

The canoe was secured offshore, and one voyageur, then another and another in order, except for Hyacinth, remained with it for an agreed time to keep it from shifting. Hyacinth got his fire going, and soon their meal was cooking. The men, lining up to receive their day's due, loosened their sashes to make room for it at such an early time. Within the hour they were paddling again, singing lustily as the colors from the sunset stained the water before them.

Dusk came, then night, and still they paddled down the center of the lake over a road Martin knew well. By midnight it was as if the sky had picked up the long-gone streamers of the sunset and was waving them from the zenith, flinging them down to the horizon, gathering them up again to hurl them across the width of the sky in ever-changing patterns. By the time a man cried, "Voilà la rose!" his companion exclaimed, "Voilà la vert!"

"C'est un bariolage," Guillaume marveled.

Hardly were the words uttered when Prosper corrected them. "It is yellow, yellow like the halos of the saints."

Hyacinth likened the colors to those of different wines, and others compared them to what they knew best. Marvelous as the colors were, they were not in the sky alone but reflected on the water. They paddled through a world of changing hues, like the heart of a rainbow or the gardens that bloomed in their songs. Martin did not call for such, nor did Guillaume find one rising within him. The night that encompassed them was singing with color, and no human voice could join in that chorus.

The aurora was not new to the voyageurs. Those who had been on many journeys into the pays d'en haut had seen it often, and Guillaume knew well its shifting radiance; but never, they said to each other in whispers, never had they seen such a display of glory, and not seen only but been a part of it. What could it mean? Martin knew, or thought he knew, but he saw no need to say. He could only press the men to more speed.

"What does it mean?"

"It means," Hypolite said, "that we have passed the Feast of St. Michael, and that worthy captain of the armies of God has taken us as his own and is directing our way."

"May he who leads us to our eternal home guide us first to our earthly one," Henri added reverently.

"St. Michael, pray for us," they chanted. The canoe moved forward through the colored water with only the sibilant sound of their praying to match the whisper made by the prow, the dip and thrust of the paddles.

Almost as suddenly as it had come, the aurora disappeared. They paddled on in the impetus and awe it had engendered until dawn began to flush over the water with a light that was no color but was day. Martin called for a pipe. Paddles were laid across gunnels to drip into the lake while Henri, in the bow, held the canoe steady so Martin might sit down and rest. Some of the men straightened their backs and raised their heads; others bent forward and leaned their heads against the nearest pièce before lighting up. Each one released cramped muscles in his own way, careful that any move made came from only the waist up.

Hyacinth took a square of pemmican from his store and gave it to Nicolet, sitting near, to break two pieces from it. It passed from one voyageur to the next one, each man breaking off what he needed or felt he could eat, for none of them knew where or when they might eat their meal of the day. The lake gave them drink, and they scooped it up to their mouths in palmfuls.

Gazing into the water, Hyacinth said: "I see fish, many fish. Tonight you shall have something more than your mush."

Martin, watching the sky, said: "I see wind rising in the east. Finish your pipes, and then we will change our course so we may have the protection of the shore."

"Saccajé chien," Hypolite muttered, "you have the eyes of a goat! You see what no one else ever can."

"Or wants to," Prosper said.

Mumbling their sacrés, they emptied and stashed their pipes, took up their paddles, and waited for direction.

"Tout à droite, lentement, lentement," Martin said, holding his long paddle still while the craft swung slowly to face the shore, then gradually swung back again to straighten course and follow down the remainder of the lake within three canoe-lengths of the shore. Their course would be more difficult, and little speed would be made since there were rocks to be avoided, and shallows. Nevertheless it would be safer, for if the wind rose quickly, they would not receive its brunt.

The day advanced toward noon, and there was small change in the light. The sun did not make an appearance. The lake was calm, unmarred by so much as a ripple until the movement of the trees along the shore proclaimed the rising wind that soon made its marks on the water.

They were approaching the end of the lake where a halt for a portage would have been called in any case when a sharp gust of wind slapped the canoe broadside and rocked it. The men turned their paddles to steady it and hold their position until Martin gave them the necessary direction. Already waves had begun to kick up in the water. It would not take many to swamp the canoe.

Martin's keen eyes had been studying the shore against such an emergency, but the only possible landing place was all of twenty canoe lengths ahead of them. He called to Henri: "This side of that great rock there is a small cove. Head us in to it, and may there be no rocks to waylay." To the men he said, "En avant et chantez"; then he added the word he rarely used, "Vite!"

Guillaume started off immediately with the chorus of the old marching song *Je Ne Suis Pas Si Vilaine*:

> " 'Cach' ton, tire, cach' ton bas,
> Cach' ton, tire, cach' ton bas,
> Cach' ton joli bas de laine,
> Car on le verra.' "

And the men put everything they had into the words and into their paddling. The song was the best for the need and the demand. It told of a young girl on her way to Varennes who met three captains who spoke to her as if she were low-born. The story might seem to have little relation to fourteen voyageurs meeting bad weather, but they sang it with rising relish. When the girl replied that she was not quite a peasant because a kingly youth was in love with her, they underscored their approval of her stand with the force in their paddle arms. The girl proved the youth's love by the gifts he had given her:

> " 'A violin of ebony,
> A rosebud beautiful to see,
> And if it flowers, queen I'll be,
> And if it fades, all peasantry.' "

Something of a similar challenge faced them: If they made the cove, the canoe and its cargo would be saved; if they did not, all would be lost.

No matter how hard they paddled, how gaily they sang, their progress was slow, for the winds and the waves increased momently and stood against their course.

"Allons, allons, mes braves gens," Martin called, not commanding so much as imploring. From where he stood in the stern he could see the distance they still had to go and the dangers there were to avoid.

Guillaume quickened the rhythm the second time through. If they had been soldiers carrying muskets and packs, they would have been going at a double trot; but they were canoemen with light clothes and slender paddles, and they had been at their posts for more than twelve hours, nor was the end in sight. Paddling with all the power they possessed, singing with all the breath in their lungs, the canoe moved slowly forward and their voices

rang above the whistling of the wind and the harsh slapping of the waves:

> " 'Cach' ton, tire, cach' ton bas,
> Cach' ton, tire, cach' ton bas,
> Cach' ton joli bas de laine,
> Car on le verra.' "

The men crouched lower. With a reserve no voyageur knew
he possessed until it was called on, paddles were thrust in
and through the water, stroke after stroke, and the craft
kept to its course.

"Bravo! Bravo!" Martin shouted. His voice carried to
each one, who knew that the safety of his comrades and
the security of the cargo depended on him alone.

They were within a canoe length of the cove when a
sudden gust of wind hit them and threw them off course,
so what had been almost within reach was now beyond
them. Being swept close to the great rock that bounded
the cove, they made a desperate effort to bring the canoe
on course and head it into the cove. Paddling too hard on
one side, balance was lost, and the canoe capsized.

Red-capped heads bobbed among the waves, arms
reached frantically for a hold on the keel of the canoe.
Coughing and spitting out water, they had no breath with
which to speak. The shore seemed a long way off.

Martin coughed out the water he had swallowed; then,
between gasps for breath, he shouted to the men, "To your
paddles—your paddles!"

The men began thrashing around in search of their
paddles. Those who could swim left the safety of the
canoe to gather up what paddles came to hand, theirs as
well as others. Some, who did not dare lose hold on the

keel, reached with one hand to grasp a paddle thrust at them while their companions continued the search. To keep the paddles from being splintered on the rocks or swept beyond reach was their immediate intent, for every one of them knew, and none better than Guillaume Puissante, that a voyageur could as well lose his right arm as his paddle.

"À la côte!" Martin shouted.

The men, clinging to the keel with one hand, clutching one or more paddles with the other, started to thrash with their feet and push the canoe toward shore. Guillaume thrust the paddle he held into Pierre's hand and dived under the craft. The water was murky and so agitated by the men's kicking that he could see little. Hand over hand along the length he felt his way to make sure that the cargo was still in place. He surfaced for breath, then dived under again and began to close his hands around some of the articles that had been loosened, mostly the small bundles of possibles and their supplies.

All fourteen voyageurs proved a match to the wind-tossed waves. Shouting, pushing, kicking, they got the canoe into shallower water. Putting their feet down, the taller ones felt sand beneath them; soon all could touch bottom. With reasonable purchase for their feet, more force could go into their arms. Partly shoving, then lifting, all hands on the gunnels, all feet on the bottom of the lake, they brought the canoe in and carried it far enough up the beach to be out of the reach of the waves; then they set it down on one side.

"Voilà le berceau!" several shouted at once, pointing to the little canoe that had not overturned.

Guillaume, last to gain the shore, with his arms filled

with an odd collection of things, saw the men looking at his little canoe. "It rocks well," he said.

And the voyageurs cheered.

Martin's eyes ran swiftly over the group as they stood by the canoe. Some were breathing hard; some were still gasping and spitting out water. With their clothes plastered to their bodies, their long hair and mustaches plastered to their skins, they looked more like fish than like men. After counting them he made another swift count: the paddles were all there, too. The cargo appeared safe, still lashed in place, but the canoe had a hole torn in its prow by the iron cook kettle when it shifted. Martin shook his head. The pièces were probably as wet as the men who had been in the water. He walked the length of the canoe, studying it, while the men waited, still too stunned by all that had happened for their usual excited palaver.

Martin sucked his lips in. Cargo could be dried; a rent could be repaired; but the price they would pay would be time. He returned to stand by the men. Each one took his cue from Martin, though he would have done likewise if left to himself. In the continuity of movement with which they boarded a canoe, they dropped to their knees on the sand and offered a prayer to Ste. Anne who had saved them from disaster. Getting to his feet, Martin called to Hyacinth and told him to fetch the keg of high wine from the stern so each man could have a dram.

"Warm your insides," Martin said after he had taken the first sip from the wooden cup and passed it to the man next to him, "then work as you have not worked since we left Montréal to unload the canoe before the storm breaks in all its fury around us."

Each went to his appointed task. Some gathered the paddles together and leaned them, blades up, against a tree, securing their position with ropes. Others carried the iron kettle and necessary food to the place designated by Hyacinth. Some gathered wood, finding sticks and logs dry enough for a blaze that would be able to consume damp wood in time. Others unloaded the sodden pièces from the canoe and stacked them in a pile that was covered with the canvas. Guillaume made sure that the bundles he had retrieved from the water were put in the hands of their rightful owners; then he inspected le petit canot. It had come through without a dent or graze. Guillaume patted it before he turned it on its side, proud of the way it was proving itself. When tasks were accomplished, the men crouched in the lee of their long canoe. It would not shed the rain from them entircly, but it broke the force of the wind. There they waited until Hyacinth called them to come to the kettle for their evening meal.

"Tomorrow, mes amis, you shall have the fish I promised you for today."

The prospect made even their familiar mush taste better. They ate well. The warmth of the food was comforting. It was good to feel their long-empty bellies pushing out against their sashes.

"Tomorrow!" Martin exclaimed. So used was he to planning the next day's march that he could scarcely think in terms of a shorebound day. "Tonight we sleep out the rain, and pray that the sun will soon shine to dry the furs."

Rain began to fall long before they had finished eating, its drops sizzling in the fire and making puddles in the food in their bowls. But rain did not dampen their spirits. Instead it seemed to heighten them. The worst that can happen to a canoe on the march had happened to them, and what of it? The cargo had not suffered, nor had they, except for a ducking in cold water. Tomorrow—morbleu! that was not upon them yet. They put their empty bowls down and started dancing around the fire, slowly at first, then more and more rapidly. Guillaume sang, and those who had breath joined in with the refrains. Any one of their paddling songs could easily become the measure for a dance; it was only a matter of mood and need. Hyacinth, stirring the kettle that there might be mush in the morning, stopped to beat time with his spoon. Martin, standing near and watching, clapped his hands. Heedless of the rain, now falling steadily, the men knew that the fiercer the storm, the sooner it would be over, and that the harder they danced, the more ready they would be to sleep.

First Pierre, then Nicolet, and lastly Hypolite left the circle of warmth and merriment and sought a place to sleep; some under the upturned canoe, others by the stack of furs; several curled up by the fire. To sleep in the rain was as much a part of their life as to paddle in the rain; but to go to sleep knowing that they had come victorious through disaster made every man feel like a king.

The sun did not come fully out until noon the next day, but once the rain had stopped there was every indication that the sun would shine. It was not luck; it was blessing, for an October storm often did not wear itself out short of three days. The wind shifted to the northwest. The lake lay calm, rippleless. The trees dripped. The ground oozed. From all the near branches hung shirts, leggings, caps, capotes as the voyageurs dried their belongings. Each man wore his sash, for without it he would have had no place to keep his pipe or from which to hang his knife. The sashes had long since dried from body warmth, and instead of hanging limp as they had the night before, swayed and fluttered as the wearers moved about their self-appointed or Martin-directed tasks.

Michel and Maurice heated tar, unstrung watap, and with a new piece of birchbark repaired the hole in the prow of the canoe. They went carefully over every seam, and added tar or renewed watap wherever there was an evidence of strain. Prosper, Jean, and Guillaume uncorded the bundles of furs and hung the pelts on every available branch, laid them over rocks, and even stretched them across the keel so they might dry out thoroughly.

Martin felt the pelts. "In time we will be able to brush them so the hair will lie smooth again," he said.

The slightest imperfection in any one of the furs, no matter how it had been caused, would bring the price down, and this could not be allowed to happen. A voyageur's wages were set when he signed on, but if the furs brought back were not in their best condition his wages could be affected, and he might have a mark against him that would not help when he wanted to sign on for another voyage. So, all fourteen men worked for the reputation of one, and each one worked for his fellows.

Skins of marten, fox, lynx, bear, otter, wolf, and muskrat all had a price, but it was beaver that commanded the highest price. The value would increase every time the pelts changed hands, first in Montréal, then in Paris or London at the great markets. At the trading post deep in the pays d'en haut, a beaver skin had been bought for a handful of glass beads; at the warehouse in Montréal it would be worth some francs; by the time it had been treated, shaped, and set on a stand in a fashionable hat shop in Paris it would be worth more than the pay a voyageur received for a whole season.

Repair work was completed on the canoe long before the pelts were dried. Each one had to be turned every few hours, like bread baking; then, when it was pronounced dry, it was brushed so that the hair looked as it had in its original state. Only then could the furs be repacked into the ninety-pound pièces and corded for loading. Martin did not chafe at what had to be and at what proved to take all of three days. That the storm had been followed soon by fair weather was as much as a man could hope for, and a fit answer to their prayers.

Moving among them and watching their work, giving a hand here or a word of advice there, Martin knew that his voyageurs would paddle all the better for the rest they were having and the change of food.

Each day Hyacinth went out in the little canoe on the lake whose waters shimmered in the sunshine. "I do not come back," he announced every time he left, "until I have a fish for every man." Nor did he.

Before the third day's sun had set, the canoe was loaded. It had been tested by the men who had taken it out on the lake, and the weight had not forced a seam or strained the patch in the prow. It would carry them and their cargo safely and well the rest of their journey. They sat around the fire for their last meal of fish and barley bread. They knew they would be on their way before dawn, but at that moment they were loath to leave the warmth of the fire and the circle of comradeship. They sang their songs, listened to each other's stories, and busied their hands whittling wood or stringing watap.

Their ears were always sharp for the unusual, as were

their eyes for the unexpected, and when they heard the sound that was as different from the waves lapping as they were from the fire whispering, sudden silence came over them and every head was lifted skyward. Searching for the makers of the sound that came out of the north, they strained to hear the faint repetitive call that meant but one thing. The sound grew stronger, clearer, nearer; then the first in a long line of migrating geese appeared over the lake. They flew high, for the sky was free of clouds. Each one was distinct, a mere dot but discernible, and the flock was a large one. As the last one went over and was lost to sight, the men sighed with release of breath. Baptiste crossed himself, and soon the others did the same.

The sound the geese made in flight continued behind them as it had preceded them, and there was no marked moment when it ceased altogether. But not until it was evident to the voyageurs sitting around the fire that the only sound to be heard was the whisper of wind through the trees of the forest did anyone speak.

"They, too, are going home."

"They, too, sing as they go."

There was not a man but whose heart was with the wild geese in their flight and whose longing to be home was like that which the geese felt for their winter home.

Their meal was finished in silence. Each one tossed his pile of fish bones into the fire, rubbed his greasy fingers clean with a last crust of bread saved for the purpose, and ran the bread over his lips before putting it into his mouth. With nothing more to eat, fingers curled around mustaches, lost themselves in long hair, before reaching for the pipe that marked the end of the meal.

Guillaume sang to them, as they smoked, the wistful

song of a shepherd to his beloved, *L'Herbe Verdit Tous les Printemps*. Listening, they nodded dreamily, each man taking it to himself in his own way. As the flowers bloomed in the spring, the geese would return to the north country; after the voyageurs had their fill of domesticity, they, too, would return to the north country. By the time Guillaume came to the last lines, the men were humming an accompaniment to the song:

> " 'L'herbe verdit tous les printemps,
>   Les fleurs aux champs se renouvellent.' "

The sun in its setting left a golden path across the lake. The men did not wait for darkness to come down, but began to seek out their sleeping places while there was still light. Wrapped in his capote, each one was soon as distant from his companions in his own world of dreams as were the southward-winging geese from them all.

Martin stirred the embers of the fire with a stick. "Sing well, Guillaume; sing well for the next few hundred miles and then you can sing to your own true love."

"We are near, then?"

"In distance, not time. The miles are hard, and there are many portages to make until we reach the river and can ride with its current."

"We will return by St. Luke's Day?"

"Peut-être que oui, peut-être que non. Say only we will return." Martin glanced up at the sky where stars were as thick as the sand at his feet.

Guillaume observed that he did not shrug his shoulders in the gesture that could mean anything. "C'est bon?"

Martin nodded. "These geese—they are flying south before the weather, and they are flying high. Every day a flock will go over, and sometimes at night you will hear them. After the last one has passed, the storms will come rolling in. We have been blessed, Guillaume, that the storm we encountered was of short duration and that it did not bring snow in its wake."

"If it had?"

Martin's shoulders went up elaborately. "We might have lost everything, and ourselves as well."

"Has it ever happened?"

"Mais oui! There are many stories that are not told by the voyageurs themselves but by their families in Montréal and the near villages whose men did not return."

As if a wind had nipped at his bare skin, Guillaume shivered and held out his hands to the warmth that still came from the embers. "Ste. Anne has us in her care."

"May she still keep watch over us," Martin said.

They sat on in silence for a while. Martin left, and after another few moments Guillaume followed him. Only Hyacinth remained near the fire, crouched in apparent sleep but readily wakeful. If the fire fell too low, he would move his hand toward a pile of light wood and toss a stick onto the embers. The stick would smolder, burst into flame, crackle, burn, and die down again. Hyacinth would keep this up until just after two o'clock, when he would stir himself, feed the fire well, and swing the big kettle over it so the morning meal would be ready for the men when he called them. A long march lay before them, and he would see that they went into it with full bellies.

When Guillaume unfolded his capote, he held the dream net in his hands and looked at it. The memories stirred by the sound of the geese going over and the approach of their own journey's end made him mindful of the time during the moon's waxing when the net had been hung over his bough bed to guard his dreams. Following an impulse, he attached the net to a low branch directly over his sleeping place; then he knelt beneath it to say his night prayers.

After le bon Dieu, Ste. Anne was the next to whom he made supplication; because St. Michael's Feast Day had so recently passed, he called upon him for protection; because his day was approaching, he called upon St. Luke. When he stretched out between the two uptwisting roots that made his bed, and drew his capote around him, he felt encompassed by an army of protectors. He was thankful that they existed and could not only be called on but relied upon. A shudder ran through his body, and he drew his covering more closely to him; but the shudder had nothing to do with the night air. It was caused by the realization that had he stayed with Willow Wand, forcing her to become his and so laying themselves open for whatever danger their desire provoked, he could not have kept his saints. If he had clung to them for a while, they would have been lost sooner or later in the vast areas to which Willow Wand addressed her thoughts—the God of the Sun, the Wind God, the Rain God, the Everywhere Spirit. These were all areas in which and by which a man lived, Guillaume knew, but they did not have the intimacy of the saints.

"Dieu merci," he whispered into the night.

At peace with himself, but far from ready for sleep, he listened to the night sounds: the heavy breathing of his comrades, the sputter when wood was thrown into the embers, the honking made by another passing flock of high-flying geese, waves lapping against the shore. The night notes were like a softly played accompaniment, and with it he sang to himself the many verses of *Le Coeur de Ma Bien-aimée*. It comforted him and gave him courage to believe that someday he would find one whose heart he could win. In the song, the gentle lady who had been so elusive had at the last been held by love. So it would be with him. Flee him, change shape as she might, someday he would lay hold of the key that would unlock her heart. He began to imagine what she would be like. Doing so, she seemed so near that he dared himself to look into the dream net and see her once for all, and so having seen, he would recognize her when they met. He drew his breath in sharply and blinked his eyes.

Looking through the circular opening in the net was the loveliest face he had ever seen: the likeness of all the maidens he had been singing about for years, yet with the distinctness of one particular maiden whose eyes saw only him. Her skin was fair. She had long golden hair, cheeks like roses, lips like ripe cherries, and eyes that were as blue as the midday sky. He spoke to her in French, and she returned his greeting. He told her how long he had sought her, and she replied, "But always I have been waiting for you." He reached for her hand to kiss her finger tips. She laughed, and the sound was like tiny bells chiming together. She put her hand to her lips and blew his kisses and her own back to him. She understood how to play the game of love and how to speak its little language first. Whatever he did she did too, but her actions added grace. He did not ask for her lips, nor did she offer them. It was still too soon.

During the night a great flight of trumpeter swans went over, their musical voices filling the air with a chorus of sound that told no story, that knew no harmony. It was part of an instinctive response to that which guided them the high way through darkness and light to their journey's end.

"Alerte, lève, lève, nos gens!" Hyacinth called, knocking on the iron kettle with his spoon.

From beside the canoe, from near the fire, from the base of big trees, forms unrolled themselves, stood up, stretched, stumbled down to the lake. Refreshed and fully awake in a matter of minutes, the men converged around the fire where bowls were already being filled from the bubbling mush in the kettle.

Guillaume lay still. He had heard the call, but he could not answer it. Gazing skyward through the dream net, he saw a spangle of stars winking through pine needles. Where was he? Where was she? He rubbed his eyes, then let his fingers slide down his cheeks and across his upper lip. Pleased at what touch told him, he smiled; then he flattened his hands over his face to cover the smile and keep close the marvel of his dream.

Usually one of the first to respond to Hyacinth's call, he was missed by the group standing around the fire putting food into their mouths as fast as Hyacinth ladled it into their bowls. "Où est Guillaume?" they asked as they looked around. They called his name into the darkness that was everywhere except in the circle of light by the fire. "Guillaume! Guillaume!"

Prosper put down his bowl and went quickly to the base of the pine tree where he knew Guillaume had his bed. When he saw him lying so still, his hands spread across his face, he feared that all was not well. "Guillaume, what is it? You are not sick, mon ami?"

Guillaume's words, coming from under his hands, had a muffled sound. "I have dreamed such a dream, Prosper, as a man may have only once in his lifetime."

"So?"

Guillaume removed his hands and smiled into the eyes of his friend. "I have seen the face of my beloved, and the sight has made me weak with longing."

Prosper spoke softly, as if to a child who must be wakened gently from his dream. "Love makes one strong, Guillaume."

Guillaume stared up and through the dream net. "Always you are right, Prosper." His tone changed. The smile no longer quivered over his lips, but stretched from ear to ear. "Go back to the fire," he said merrily, "but see that Hyacinth saves enough for me to have my bowl filled twice. I am strong, but I would be stronger."

"Bien." Prosper's relief made him practical. "We have many miles to go today; there will be need for many songs." He returned to the fire to assure the men that their singer would soon be with them.

The voyageurs raised their bowls with a lusty cheer and resumed their eating, their boasting, their laying of bets. Hyacinth pretended to look disgusted. To Martin he said: "It is a waste of a good thing ever to give those men high wine. Look at them! They are drunk as a table of kings."

"Drunk with the prospect of a day's work," Martin replied. "Eheu, Hyacinth, it is not good to be idle for long."

Guillaume reached for the dream net, freed it from the branch on which it had hung through the night, and kissed it; then he folded it into his capote, vowing that he would not part with it until he met the one whose face fitted as perfectly within its rim as had the face he had seen in his dream. He went down to the lake to wash. The cold water that drove sleep from his eyes did not drive away the dream: a glow from it continued to envelop him.

Cupping water in his hands, he tried to hold it because of the stars it reflected. The water slipped through his fingers; but always there was more where it came from, and stars in the sky to shine in it, however briefly. He drank to Monsieur le Comte who had given him words that, like the medal of a saint, had protected him. He drank to Prosper who had told him to wait for the best, that it would surely come. Then, cupping his hands a third time and bringing the lake to his lips, he drank to his bien-aimée.

What was her name—Hélène, Marguerite, Jeanne? Names in the songs he sang came through his mind. Celeste. Ah, that would be a name for her, come from heaven as all good must come. She was real, but of course she was real: otherwise, how could she have come to him in his dream? He talked to himself as if he were his friend. "Guillaume Puissante, how was it that you doubted?"

He joined his comrades by the fire and ate well; then he tightened his sash.

"Allons, we go forward!" Martin called.

The already loaded canoe was lifted and carried into the water, pushed out until it could float and be boarded. The men leaped to their places, held their paddles high while waiting for the word. The surface of the lake was mottled with the reflections of stars. The east, into which their prow faced, looked no different from the west, for dawn would not give even a hint for another hour. Martin's eyes took in the position of the cargo, the men crouched with paddles poised, le petit canot safely cordelled behind the stern. He glanced toward the shore that had been their safe haven, at the fire smoldering from the water that had been poured on it. All was as it should be. The past was behind. The future was theirs.

"En avant!" Martin shouted.

Paddle blades clipped the water. The canoe, like an arrow shot from an invisible bow, went forward, its direction sure, its passage swift.

" 'En roulant ma boule,' " Guillaume began.

The words rang out brave and clear; soon supported by a chorus of thirteen other voices, the sound reached across the dark lake, echoing against its far shore.

They sang the dawn in; they sang the sun up the sky; they sang themselves to the end of the lake and their first portage, where Martin called for a pipe.

"Allumez," he said. Paddles were secured; hands reached into sashes for pipes, into sacs-à-feu for tobacco. The canoe rocked at ease.

Once onto and over the portage, they sang themselves to the next portage, and so the long day went, interspersed with pipes and poses, terminated by food and rest. That night, when Guillaume unfolded his capote, he left the dream net on the moss beside his sleeping place. The next morning he packed it again in his capote. This was his procedure during all the nights that remained of the journey. He had seen all that he needed. He did not want to see her again in a dream, but find her in life. If he did not find her in Montréal, he would look for her in Québec.

"Where is a beautiful maiden to be found?" he asked Prosper during a pipe.

"À Saint-Malo, à Nantes, peut-être à Paris."

"But those places are in the songs we sing!" Guillaume protested.

"So are the beautiful maidens."

Guillaume was silent.

"Beauty, what is it?" Prosper asked, though not of Guillaume or of anyone within reach of his voice. "A woman who can dance and sing with you, who can make a potage that gives you strength and can use her hands about the house, who can fill the cradle now and then, is she not beautiful? Ah—" Prosper's long sigh was followed by quiet. The far-off expression on his face told of where his thoughts were. Often he voiced his thoughts; this time he guarded them. A man might talk and boast of love, but when it came to the love of which he alone knew all, only his silence could give it fitting sanctity.

On the Rue de Souris, under the shadow of Mount Royal, was a stone house with three rooms that had seen much living. It had always been the right size, either when it was crowded with children or as it was now when a woman grown large and rheumatic lived in it alone much of the year. Her cheeks were creased with lines; her dark hair was streaked with gray; but there was no one in all Montréal who could make a potage to match hers. Even now she might be making one against the homecoming of the wiry little voyageur whose legs were bandied from the position he sat in so often, whose shoulders were stooped from the heavy loads he carried, whose skin was creased by the weather, and whose joints could, in the winter, creak as did hers.

The children who had filled the house and kept her busy during the months her man was away had all gone —many to death, for death seemed to have a special fondness for little children. Some had gone to adventure and some to love. So the two were back where they had started, and when they sat out the long winter together by the warm stove it would be as it had been so many years ago after the priest had made them man and wife, and before the cradle had its first occupant.

"Ah—" Prosper breathed again, but further words were lost in his dreaming.

"She is beautiful, then?" Guillaume pressed eagerly.

"As a turtledove, as a roe deer, as a flower in spring." All these he had sung about, and he knew of nothing more beautiful with which to compare her.

They were riding the current of the great river now, and the weather held no threat. Even Martin could say with assurance that they would be in Montréal soon. "Bientôt."

"Demain?" they pressed him.

"Bientôt," he repeated. Beyond his first assurance he would not commit himself. There could still be delays, and danger was something of which he never ceased to be aware until cargo, canoe, and voyageurs were all back in Montréal.

Prosper held up his hands and counted three fingers. Two he turned back into his palm, one he left upright. "On the third day from now I shall be with her."

"God willing."

"Of nothing, mon ami, is He more willing than that those who love should be together."

Guillaume could not say. He did not know. He could only hope.

For the next three days a strong sun lorded it in the sky, and a good west wind aided the momentum gained from

the current. As paddles flashed and voices sang, the miles
sped by. Familiar landmarks began to appear when the
forest gave way to fields where animals grazed and crops
had been harvested. People looked up from their work to
wave and join in with the voyageurs' song as the canoe
went by.

"Bravo!" they cried. They had been counting them all,
and now the last of the brigade was in the home river.

At Ste. Anne's shrine the canoe turned toward shore
and was held still while the voyageurs offered their devo-
tion and their thanks. Late though they were, the cargo
was safe, and every one of the fourteen men who had
paddled up the river on that May morning a lifetime ago
was paddling back again. They raised their paddles from
the water and tipped them in salute to their patron, then
turned the craft slowly toward the east.

"Alouette—" their song rang out.

Chapter Twelve

THE EASE AND merriment of the men on the river was not shared by their people in Montréal. All during the first two weeks in October the nine other canoes that made up the brigade had been arriving back with their cargoes of furs and their men, each one with a string of stories that would keep his family open-eyed for weeks to come. Only a voyageur knew the rigorous routine of the marches, the bone-weariness of the portages, the short nights, the dull food; but only a voyageur could make it sound as if the past five months had been one long gala day: paddling across wide lakes, threading narrow rivers, running cascades, camping beneath great trees. No one asked a returning voyageur if the journey had been hard, for the answer would have been a shrug of the shoulders and an exclamation such as, "Mais, c'est la vie!" A rollicking laugh would have followed as a story was begun that would be added to, embellished, improved upon, and rarely concluded until the time came for the canoes to leave again for the pays d'en haut.

When St. Luke's Day passed, concern for the Number Three canoe changed to anxiety; and as the days went by, it mounted. St. Luke's Day was the day when the brigades should be accounted for, the furs stored in the warehouse, the canoes carried to their winter storage; for beyond that day the weather could not be trusted. It might be fair for weeks; it could become winter overnight.

Word traveled swiftly, though not always accurately, and as the different canoes arrived at Lachine they brought variants of news that added to the growing apprehension. One of the brigade had seen Martin's men arriving at the trading post in July just as they were departing, and reported that the canoe with a full-faced sun on its prow was short a man. Where a voyageur should have been sitting were two corded pièces, one on top of the other. When the question was asked which of the men was missing—was it Martin? Henri? Guillaume? Prosper? Michel? Hyacinth? Hypolite? Nicolet?—the informant could not say.

The next to the last canoe to leave Grand Portage told of being sung on their way by Martin's men who, at the time of their departure, had appeared at the top of Mount Rose.

"Were there seven men or eight?"

"Ah, that no one of us could say. The distance was great. There were many trees. But they sang well."

One story, then another, was told, and the question remained for all to ponder: Why was the Number Three so late? The only possible answer was that they must be a man short, for one voyageur less could alter the speed of a canoe and the distance traversed, no matter how hard the others worked. Laurent brought in a story that was more confusing and distressing than any of the others. Somewhere on the chain of lakes traveled by the north canoes, his canoe had sighted the one with the vermilion sun.

"Behind it, a little canoe was riding the waves!"

"You saw it, with your own eyes?"

"Mais oui, but it was at a great distance."

"How large was the canoe in tow?"

Laurent flung his arms wide. "Perhaps twice my reach, but no more. It was hardly big enough for a child to handle."

"But big enough for an Indian girl to hide in," one of Laurent's companions said, shaking his head.

"Or big enough to carry a dead man wrapped small in his capote," Laurent added grimly.

The stories told at the dock and repeated on the wharf near the warehouse found their way to the city, and there they grew as they went up one street and down another, through a keyhole at one house and out its chimney to enter the next house blacker and more woeful. The women steeled themselves for tragedy, but each one lived in the hope that it might not be hers. For one more day they would speak in full voices and go briskly about their affairs, as tomorrow everything might be changed. Familiar with grief, they knew that it had to be accepted and could be borne, and that life would resume its course even though something had gone from it. The empty chair at the table would soon cease to reproach; the shirt made to replace one worn out by the summer could be put away until a son grew big enough to call it his. Only the numbness would remain.

Five months was a long time to be without a man, and now each day was like a week. They hungered for the embrace of rough arms so used to handling canoes that they treated their women like them; they yearned for the sound of voices that had sung so long they scarcely knew how to speak. And they knew from years past how good it would be to have a man's footsteps in the house again, even though they might be like a cat's from the balancing of heavy loads over perilous ground. They had waited a long time and, if there was any truth in the stories brought in by the returning voyageurs about Martin's canoe, one of their number might go on waiting.

They made frequent trips to the church to pray, each one for her man's safe return. Words were not sufficient; candles must be lit to get the attention of a patron saint who might, at this juncture, be able to do more than Ste. Anne or St. Luke or St. Michael; but candles cost a sou apiece, and there were not many sous left by now in the households whose men had not returned.

On the twenty-first day of October, Bénédict Beaulieu sat in his office near the wharf at Montréal. He was surrounded by piles of prime pelts, and the air had a strong animal smell; but it was a smell Bénédict reveled in, for it meant the season had been good. And, what was more, it meant that his report to La Compagnie Pelleterie in Paris would be worth reading and his coffers would be full of louis d'or. When the smell from the furs got to be more than he could relish, he took his pipe from the table, filled it with tobacco, and enveloped himself in smoke; then he returned to the lists he was making of the furs brought in by the returning canoes. There was a winter's work ahead in sorting them, labeling and packing, before they would be ready to be sent to France on the first vessel to sail in the spring when ice went out of the river. Bénédict sighed. Now and then there was a voyageur who wanted to do something more than sleep through the winter. He would hire one or two such to work with him on the furs. But he had hired one already, he reminded himself.

Last April, when he had been signing on voyageurs, he had engaged one who could write his own name, Guillaume Puissante. He had promised him work for the winter, and a home as well. Bénédict's eyes studied the sheet of paper on the table before him. It gave the names of the men on the Number Three canoe, the canoe that had not yet been reported in, and one of the names was that of Guillaume Puissante.

In spite of the furs surrounding him and the smoke enveloping him, Bénédict could feel the thrust of the wind as it came off the river and rattled the windows of the warehouse. It was cold; it would soon be colder. No matter how brightly the sun might shine, the knife edge of winter could be felt. Bénédict puffed on his pipe. He was getting old, he told himself; that was why he felt the cold.

A sudden imperious knocking sounded on the door.

"Entrez," he growled.

The door was pushed open. It was a runner from Lachine. Breathing hard, he found his way around the piles of furs to the table where Bénédict sat.

"Monsieur Bénédict, the canoe—has been—sighted —in the river!"

Bénédict waved the drift of his smoke away so he could the better see his messenger. "What canoe?"

"The Number Three canoe, Monsieur Bénédict, the one we have all been waiting for."

Bénédict rose to his feet and peered over the head of the young man and out the open door. "C'est vrai?"

The runner nodded, forcing his breath to come slowly so he could give the information with which François had entrusted him. "C'est vrai, Monsieur Bénédict. With my own eyes I saw them—all fourteen paddles were raised in salute. The canoe—it was riding low. It must have a great weight of furs."

"You saw this?"

"Yes, yes, Monsieur Bénédict, I saw and I heard—even at a distance—even above the roar of the rapids—we heard them singing."

"What were they singing?"

" 'En roulant ma boule roulant.' "

Bénédict wagged his head. "Mais naturellement! They sing coming back what they sang when they went out."

"You have a message for François, Monsieur Bénédict?"

Bénédict sat down heavily. "Why should I have a message for him? He knows what to do. He has done it with nine other canoes."

"He said—"

"But of course I have a message! Tell him to send the men to me tout de suite. Unloading can be done tomorrow. Those who reach this office before sunset will receive their pay."

"Bien."

"What are you standing there for? Sacré bleu, have you no feet to get you on your way or tongue to deliver my words?"

The runner turned and left the office.

Bénédict sat back in his chair, laid down his pipe, took a large silk handkerchief from his pocket, and slowly mopped his face. He had known all along, he told himself, that the Number Three canoe was safe and would return with its cargo and all its men; he had known, no matter what rumor had said. Had not he told the foolish women that, when they flocked every day to his office to ask for news? Had not he told them that Martin was the best steersman in all New France and that no one could equal Henri in the bow? Had not he told them that Hyacinth's cooking could please the King in Paris? And had not he said that the chanteur in the Number Three canoe was the ablest he had heard in many a year? And what had they done but say to him that the chanteur had no woman to return to and that was not good.

"It is bad luck," they had said, "for a man to go to the pays d'en haut and not have a woman to whom he must come back."

"Allez, allez," he had said to them, while muttering imprecations enough to frighten the Devil himself, "Guillaume Puissante has more women than I have fingers on one hand."

They said nothing, for they knew better. When they left him, some went to the church to light another candle, and others went home to stir the soup.

Bénédict folded his handkerchief and put it back in his pocket. He glanced up at the clock on the wall, studying it as the pendulum swung back and forth, back and forth, back and forth. Making allowance for the time the runner had taken and the distance of the canoe from Lachine, as well as the time it would take for the men to walk from the dock at Lachine to his office on the wharf at Montréal, Bénédict determined that it would be close to sunset when they would arrive.

"Tina!" he called to his granddaughter, who was in the house that adjoined the office. When she did not immediately appear he called again, "*Tina!*"

Leaving the work she was doing to answer his summons, Tina stood in the doorway of the office. "Pépé?"

"A runner has come from Monsieur François. You may go and tell the women that the canoe has been seen."

She clapped her hands to her mouth; but though she might stifle an exclamation, nothing could cover the smile that spread across her face. "Le troisième canot?"

"There was no other to arrive." Bénédict ruffled the papers on his table. "Tell the women to come here at sunset if they would see their men and lay hold on the pay before the men start spending it."

"Oui, Pépé." She approached the table and stood with her hands against it.

"Tell the women they are not to go to Lachine; they will only clutter the road. They are to come here. Ici, ici," he slapped his hand on the table. "Do you understand?"

"Oui, Pépé." Tina made no move.

He peered up at her. "What is the matter with you? Why do you not do what I say?"

"Pépé, are all the men—all the men—"

"Fourteen paddles were raised in salute. Their singing could be heard."

"Singing? Above the roar of the rapids?"

"Naturellement! Guillaume Puissante is their chanteur."

Bénédict did not look at his granddaughter now; he stared at her. So used had he been to thinking of her as a little girl that he had almost forgotten she would grow to be a woman. He saw that she was smiling, but also that there were tears on her cheeks.

"Tina, Tina," he said half reproachfully, half warningly, "you knew that canoe would come back."

"Naturellement!" she exclaimed, tossing her head high. "It was I who gave the chanteur his sash."

She ran around the table that separated her from her grandfather and put her arms around him, "C'est bon, Pépé; c'est très, très bon!" Then she hurried back to her kitchen.

After she had gone, Bénédict found himself humming the tune of an old, old song, *V'Là l'Bon Vent!*

Though Tina had a pot of soup on the stove, she knew that if a young man was to be fed as well as her grandfather, she would need to add another marrowbone and a cabbage from the garden. First she must tell the women the good news they had long been awaiting. Flinging a shawl over her shoulders, she ran singing out of the house.

Long before sunset the women gathered on the wharf near the office to await the arrival of their men. Two held infants who would see their fathers for the first time; several small children, who had forgotten what a father was, were curious and kept badgering their mothers with questions; others, older and more carefree, played games round and about the women's full skirts. Wind coming off the river was cold. A few of the women held their shawls tightly about them, but most were too eager and impatient to notice the weather.

It was well the women were early, for the men were, too. Long before they could be seen on the road from Lachine, their voices could be heard; sound preceded sight as once it had followed sight. Lustily, gaily, they sang as they marched home; they had sung in the same manner when they marched away more than five months ago. Around a bend in the road they came, arms swinging except for the arms that held the bundles of possibles. Only one carried something on his back, a canoe that might have been made for a child. They were as ragged a band of men as had ever returned from the pays d'en haut. Shirts were torn, sashes frayed, red caps on all but one of the heads were faded from the summer sun. Most of the caps flaunted feathers, but even they had become bedraggled. Gaunt and spare the men looked, brown and cheerful. Each woman sought for the face of her own, and with aching heart and speechless lips waited. Suddenly the men started running: each one to the arms held out for him.

Guillaume watched, sharing the men's joy as he had shared with them danger and drudgery, pleasure and privation; then he went toward the office. He would be able to collect his pay and have a word or two with Monsieur Bénédict Beaulieu before the others came pouring in. He leaned the small canoe against the doorjamb, took the bundle wrapped in his capote, and went up to the door.

It was opened for him by a smiling-faced girl who looked familiar even though he was sure he had never seen her before. She was no taller than he, but much plumper; her straw-colored hair was done in neat braids that, instead of resting on her shoulders, were coiled over her ears; her cheeks were flushed as if she had been bending over a fire; her eyes were blue; her lips parted at sight of him.

"Guillaume! Guillaume Puissante!" she exclaimed. "Sois-tu le bien-venu!"

He bowed his head and reached instinctively for the cap that was not there. He took her hand and held it to his lips. When he looked at her again, he smiled and said, "Oui, je suis Guillaume, mais vous, mademoiselle, qui êtes-vous?"

"Have you forgotten me, Guillaume? I, who gave you your sash?" She put her hands on it and pulled him into the office. "I am Tina, Bénédict's Tina."

At that moment Bénédict approached and, thrusting his granddaughter aside, went toward Guillaume and put his arms around him. He kissed him on one cheek and the other, then held him at arms' length for a better view. "So, you are back and you are grown! But you are thin, Guillaume Puissante; it will give Tina much work to do to put some flesh on your bones."

Tina laughed and edged herself forward again. "What have you brought to me, Guillaume?"

Outside, in the open space between the river and the warehouse, the men could be seen undoing their bundles, taking from them the small trinkets they had traded or fashioned, or come by in some way for their women. Tina, watching the smiles on the faces of the women, the gallant gestures of the men as they presented their gifts, was curious as to what Guillaume had for her in the bundle under his arm.

"Eheu!" Bénédict exclaimed, "is it not enough to have him home with us? What more do you want?"

"But—" Guillaume looked from Bénédict to Tina. At that moment he was so charmed by the pretty pout on her lips and the droop of her lashes on her cheeks that he felt he would have given her his life had she asked for it.

Bénédict laughed. "You do not know her? Ah, well, she has grown. Time does that to us all. With you, you grow up. With me"—he slapped his ample stomach—"I grow round. She is a good cook, Guillaume; she can make much out of little, my Tina can."

"Pépé, s'il te plaît!"

"Pardon, mademoiselle," he said to her; then he winked slyly at Guillaume. "Now that she is grown up, she wants me to call her Celestine."

Guillaume drew in his breath, and stared. Why had he not known? Of course he had seen that face before, rimmed by the dream net.

Bénédict turned away and started back to his table. "Your money is counted out, Guillaume. I have work for you to do tomorrow and a place for you to sleep tonight."

"Merci, m'sieu," Guillaume said, scarcely knowing what his words were. "Celestine," he murmured. He took her hand again and held it to his lips. This time he did not release it, but looked at her over it, speaking to her with his eyes.

"C'est bien," she murmured, and retrieved her hand. Her eyes rested on the bundle in his other hand. "But you do have something for me, don't you Guillaume?"

"Mais bien sûr!"

Putting his bundle on the floor, he knelt beside it, unfolded his capote, and took from it the dream net. She watched him, wondering what it was that he had. Never had she seen its like before.

Guillaume stood up straight with the wooden circlet in both hands. He held it carefully before her. With a gesture worthy of Monsieur le Comte, he bowed and presented it to her.

She accepted it with a movement of her head and a ripple of thanks running over her lips. It was a delicate, fragile thing, and beautiful in its own mysterious way. She turned it in her hands, awed as much as she was puzzled by it.

Guillaume watched her.

She put it up to her head, and laughed. "Ce n'est pas un chapeau?"

"No, it is not a hat."

She studied it again. "Surely it is not a strainer for the soup? Too much would go through that hole."

Now Guillaume was the one to laugh. "Non, non, ce n'est pas pour le potage."

She turned it round and round in her hands. Her expression began to lose its puzzlement as if the dream net were in some way communicating itself to her. She held it up to her face and looked through the center opening. "It is for me to see you better."

"Or for me to see you." He gazed at her as if it were the second time in his life that he had seen her, for her face was framed by the circle, and it was the face he had seen in his dream. "Celestine!" he exclaimed. He took her hand again and held it. There was no more for him to say: his heart had found its home.

"Merci, Guillaume," she murmured. She knew that the gift was precious to him and that in giving it to her he had done her honor. "You will tell me what it means?"

"Yes, I shall tell you."

From the far end of the room Bénédict called testily, "Guillaume Puissante, come here and let me settle with you; then Tina can go to join the women."

"Pépé, I must tend to my soup. Guillaume will be hungry."

"Go to your soup, then. Ah, me, ah, me, always with a woman it is her potage, as if nothing else mattered."

Tina tossed her head, but before she left Guillaume for the kitchen her eyes gave him an answer to the question in his own. Watching her go, holding the dream net above her head as if it were a crown, he knew that the little game of love now had two to play it.

"I come, Monsieur Bénédict," Guillaume called as he moved down the room between the piles of furs.

"Voilà!" Monsieur Bénédict said, gesturing with both hands.

Guillaume stood by the table where coins had been arranged in piles of different heights. There were four piles that were twice as high as the remaining ten.

"Pour Martin, pour Henri, pour Hyacinth," Bénédict said, and then, as he pushed the last pile away from him, "pour Guillaume."

Guillaume looked at the coins that seemed, just then, like the wealth of the world. He took them one by one and slipped them into his sac-à-feu that was now empty except for the fire steel in its bottom. "Merci, m'sieu." Sure of their safety, he looked across the table at Monsieur Bénédict. "I do not know, m'sieu, how this can be—"

"You have earned it, Guillaume; you were the chanteur."

"Non, non, Monsieur Bénédict, how can it be that little Tina has become Celestine?"

Bénédict Beaulieu wagged his head. "Ah—" The sound was heavy with memory. "A girl soon becomes a woman, Guillaume, when her heart is in her hands. Now go, you have your due. Make way for the others."

Guillaume stood aside as the voyageurs came swarming in the door, some with arms still wrapped around their wives, others with children clustering about their legs and hampering their steps. Hypolite had already been pressed into service as he tried to quiet the wailing baby in his arms, and Nicolet was wiping the nose of a small girl with the tattered end of his ceinture fléchée. Guillaume scarcely knew them, so different had they become.

Martin, who had always given the orders that his men had followed, was meekly following a woman who was determined to get her hands first on the money due him. Hyacinth could hardly be seen for the twin boys who rode on his shoulders and played their hands in his long hair. Henri was carrying in his arms a little girl who was fast asleep. But Prosper, where was he? Guillaume searched among the men, eager to see for himself the one who had been likened to everything beautiful in the songs.

He peered around a pile of furs, then another, and finally went back to the door, thinking that Prosper and his bien-aimée might still be on the wharf. He saw them at the doorway. Prosper was deeply embraced in a temporary farewell; his woman was so large that only with difficulty would she have been able to move in the crowded warehouse.

"C'est bien." Guillaume smiled, not wanting to disturb them.

Aware now of the smell of the potage that was coming from the kitchen and that was stronger than the odor of the furs or the smoke from the pipes or of the people, Guillaume turned away quickly and went toward the door that led into the house.

"En avant!" he said, though no one heard him in the babble. Forward: that was the one direction in which a voyageur could go.

Some Songs of the Voyageurs

En Roulant Ma Boule

A-ROLLING MY BOWL

Der rier' chez_nous y-a-t un é - tang; Rou-li-te rou-lant Ma bou - le rou-lant. Trois ca-nards blancs s'en vont_bai-gnant. Rou-li - te rou-lant, Bou - le rou-lant, En rou - lant ma bou -le qui rou-le, En rou-lant ma bou - le.—

En Roulant Ma Boule

1   Derrier' chez nous   y-a-t un étang;
    Roulite roulant
    Ma boule roulant.
  Trois canards blancs   s'en vont baignant.
    Roulite roulant,
    Boule roulant,
    En roulant ma boule
    Qui roule,
    En roulant ma boule.

223

2   Trois canards blanc   s'en vont baignant.
    Roulite roulant
        Ma boule roulant.
    Le fils du roi   s'en va chassant,
        Roulite roulant,
            Boule roulant,
        En roulant ma boule
            Qui roule,
        En roulant ma boule.

3   Le fils du roi   s'en va chassant,
    Avec son grand   fusil d'argent.

4   Avec son grand   fusil d'argent.
    Visa le noir,   tua le blanc.

5   Visa le noir,   tua le blanc.
    "O fils du roi,   tu es méchant!

6   "O fils du roi,   tu es méchant!
    Tu as tu-é   mon canard blanc.

7   Tu as tu-é   mon canard blanc.
    Par ses deux yeux   sort'nt les diamants,

8   Par ses deux yeux   sort'nt les diamants,
    Et par son bec   l'or et l'argent,

9   Et par son bec   l'or et l'argent,
    Et par sous l'aile   il perd son sang.

10 Et par sous l'aile   il perd son sang,
    Et tout's ses plum's   s'en vont au vent.

11 Et tout's ses plum's   s'en vont au vent.
    Y sont trois dam's   les ramassant;

12 Y sont trois dam's   les ramassant;
    Et nous ferons   un lit de camp;

13 Et nous ferons   un lit de camp;
    Nous coucherons   tous deux dedans,

14 Nous coucherons   tous deux dedans,
    Et nous aurons   des p'tits enfants;

15　Et nous aurons　des p'tits enfants;
　　Nous en aurons　des p'tits, des grands."

A-ROLLING MY BOWL

1　Behind our cabin's a little lake,
　　A-roly pololy,
　　　My bowlie rowlie.
　　Two ducks go bathing and a drake,
　　A-roly pololy,
　　　Bowlie rowlie,
　　　Rolling my bowl
　　　For to roll,
　　A-rolling my bowl.

2　Three white-feather ducks a-bathing go,
　　A-roly pololy,
　　　My bowlie rowlie.
　　The prince he comes with a gun and a bow.
　　A-roly pololy,
　　　Bowlie rowlie,
　　　Rolling my bowl
　　　For to roll,
　　A-rolling my bowl.

3　The son of the king, the king his son,
　　He comes to hunt with a silver gun.

4　With his gun of silver, silver-bright,
　　Took aim at the black and killed the white.

5　His aim was black and white the duck.
　　"O son of the king, you have wicked luck.

6　"You are very wicked, O son of the king,
　　Killing my duck was a wicked thing,

7　"My duck you've killed, my duck was white."
　　His eyes are a-gleam with diamonds bright.

225

8   Oh from his eyes the diamonds leak,
    Gold and silver from his beak,

9   His beak is dripping golden rings,
    And blood is dripping from his wings,

10 The white duck's wings are dripping blood,
    The wind is white with feather-flood,

11 With all his feathers the wind is thick.
    Three ladies gather up and pick,

12 Three ladies gather the feather yield.
    "And we shall make us a bed in the field,

13 "A feather bed we'll gather and heap,
    For two to snuggle, two to sleep.

14 "We'll sleep on a bed of white duck's feather,
    Little children have together,

15 "Little children will befall,
    Children big and children small."

Le Coeur de Ma Bien-aimée

THE HEART OF MY WELL-BELOVED

J'ai fait u - ne maî -tres - se, y a pas long -

temps. J'ai fait u - ne maî -tres - se, y a pas long - temps. —

— J'i-rai la voir di - man - che, ah oui, j'i -

rai. La de-mande à m'a - mie je lui fe - rai.

Le Coeur de Ma Bien-aimée

1 J'ai fait une maîtresse, y a pas longtemps. (*bis*)
J'irai la voir dimanche, ah oui, j'irai!
La demande à m'amie je lui ferai.

2 "Si tu y viens dimanche, je n'y s'rai pas. (*bis*)
Je me mettrai anguille, sous un rocher.
De moi tu n'auras pas mes amitiés."

3 "Si tu te mets anguille, sous un rocher, (*bis*)
Je me mettrai pêcheure, pour te pêcher.
Je pêcherai le cœur d'ma bien-aimé'."

4 "Si tu te mets pêcheure, pour me pêcher, (*bis*)
Je me mettrai gazelle, dedans un champ.
De moi tu n'auras pas d'contentement."

5 "Si tu te mets gazelle, dedans un champ, (*bis*)
Je me mettrai chasseure, pour te chasser.
Je chasserai le cœur d'ma bien-aimé'."

227

6 "Si tu te mets chasseure,   pour me chasser, (*bis*)
Je me mettrai nonette,   dans un couvent.
De moi tu n'auras pas   d'contentement."

7 "Si tu te mets nonette,   dans un couvent, (*bis*)
Je me mettrai prêcheure,   pour te prêcher.
Je prêcherai le cœur   d'ma bien-aimé'."

8 "Si tu te mets prêcheure,   pour me prêcher, (*bis*)
Je me mettrai étoile,   au firmament.
De moi tu n'auras pas   d'contentement."

9 "Si tu te mets étoile,   au firmament, (*bis*)
Je me mettrai nuage,   pour te cacher.
Je cacherai le cœur   d'ma bien-aimé'."

10 "Si tu te mets nuage,   pour me cacher, (*bis*)
Je me mettrai en vierge,   au paradis.
De moi tu n'auras pas   d'contentement."

11 "Si tu te mets en vierge,   au paradis, (*bis*)
Je me mettrai saint Pierre,   j'aurai les clefs.
Et j'ouvrirai le cœur   d'ma bien-aimé'."

THE HEART OF MY WELL-BELOVED

1 A gentle lady charmed me, not long ago. (*bis*)
I'll visit her on Sunday; it shall be so,
I'll make my lady fair say "yes" or "no."

2 "But if you come on Sunday, I'll not be there. (*bis*)
Beneath a rock half-hidden I'd be an eel,
Your wish would not be gained. No love I'd feel."

3 "If as an eel you're hidden, under a rock, (*bis*)
Then I shall be an angler, angling for you.
I'll angle for your heart till it prove true."

4 "If you become an angler angling for me, (*bis*)
I'll be a little roe deer roaming the land,
And though you seek my love, you'll seek in vain."

5   "If you become a roe deer, roaming the land, *(bis)*
     I'll chase you as a hunter over the plain,
     Until I come at last your heart to gain."

6   "If you become a hunter scouring the plain, *(bis)*
     A nun inside a convent cloistered I'll be.
     Then certainly you'll taste no joy of me."

7   "A nun inside a convent if you become, *(bis)*
     Then I'll become a preacher, preaching to you.
     I'll preach and teach your heart how love is true."

8   "If you become a preacher, preaching to me *(bis)*
     I'll be a star in heaven, lost in the blue.
     Where I can never give comfort to you."

9   "Were you a star in heaven, lost in the blue, *(bis)*
     I'd be a little cloudlet covering you,
     I'd whisper in your heart, how love is true."

10   "Were you a little cloudlet covering me, *(bis)*
     To Paradise I'd hide me, unmated yet,
     And still in spite of all, no joy you'd get."

11   "Though Paradise receive you, unmated yet, *(bis)*
     Then I shall be Saint Peter, I'll take my key
     And I'll unlock your heart, then you'd love me."

Le Bâtiment Merveilleux

THE WONDERFUL BOAT

Ce sont les gens de Bou-cher-vill', Se sont fait faire un bât - i - ment. Se sont fait faire un bâ - ti - ment, Pour al - ler jou - er de - dans. Gai - lon - là, __ bru - net - te! Gai - lon - là ____ gai - ment.

Le Bâtiment Merveilleux

1   Ce sont les gens de Boucherville
    Se sont fait faire un bâtiment (*bis*)
    Pour aller jouer dedans.
      Gailonlà, brunette!
      Gailonlà, gaîment!

2   La charpent' du bâtiment,
    C'est un' boite de fer blanc.
    Les trois mats du bâtiment,
    Sont trois cotons d'herb' Saint-Jean.

3   Le gouvernail du bâtiment,
    C'est la queue d'un vieux ch'val blanc.
    Les trois voil's du bâtiment,
    Sont trois vest's de bouragan.

230

4 Le capitain' du bâtiment,
   C'est un vieux bœuf au front tout blanc.
   La cuisinièr' du bâtiment,
   C'est un' vach de trente-cinq ans.

5 L'équipag' du bâtiment,
   Ce sont des agneaux du printemps,
   Et tous ceux qui vont dedans,
   Ce sont de vrais innocents!

THE WONDERFUL BOAT

1 The worthy folk of Butcher-town,
   Determined they would build a boat;
   Determined they would build a boat,
   And would have some fun afloat.
   Gailonlà, brunette,
   Gailonlà, gaîment!

2 They made a start upon the hull:
   For it an old tin box sufficed;
   Three stalks of mugwort furnished masts
   Rigged with halyards badly spliced.

3 The wondrous rudder was the tail
   That once adorned an old white horse.
   The sails that fluttered on the masts,
   Three ton shirts of fustian coarse.

4 The captain of that man-of-war,
   An old white-frontaled bull was he.
   The cook that served that man-of-war
   Was a cow aged thirty-three.

5 The crew were little springtide lambs
   That gaily gamboled fore and aft.
   And everyone aboard that ship
   Was quite definitely daft.

231

Alouette!

AH! THE LARK

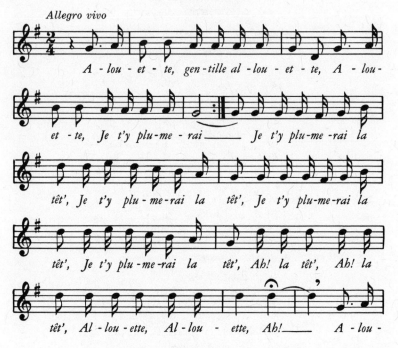

Alouette!

1 Alouette, gentille alouette,
  Alouette, je t'y plumerai. (*bis*)
    Je t'y plumerai la têt', (4 *fois*)
      Ah! la têt', (*bis*)
      Alouette, (*bis*)
      Ah!

2 Alouette, gentille alouette,
  Alouette, je t'y plumerai. (*bis*)
    Je t'y plumerai le bec, (4 *fois*)
      Et le bec, (*bis*)
      Et la têt' (*bis*) . . .

232

... Je t'y plumerai les yeux ...
Et les yeux,
Et le bec,
Et la têt' ...

Etc.: le cou, les ailes, le dos,
les pattes, la queue ...

AH! THE LARK

1 Ah! the lark, gentille alouette!
Ah! the lark, I'll pluck your feathers! (*bis*)
I'll pluck feathers off your head. (*4 times*)
Ah! the head, (*bis*)
Ah! the lark, (*bis*)
Ah!

2 Ah! the lark, gentille alouette!
Alouette, I'll pluck your feathers! (*bis*)
I'll pluck feathers off your bill. (*4 times*)
Ah! the bill ...

Etc.: the neck, the wings, the back, the legs, the tail ...

Le Miracle du Nouveau-Né

THE MIRACLE OF THE NEWBORN CHILD

Sont trois fau-cheurs de-dans les prés;— Sont trois fau-cheurs de-dans— les— prés; Trois jeu-nes fill' vont y— fa-ner.— Je suis jeune;— j'en-tends les bois re-ten-tir; Je suis jeune et jo-lie.—

Le Miracle du Nouveau-Né

1 Sont trois faucheurs   dedans les prés; (*bis*)
   Trois jeunes fill'   vont y faner.
   Je suis jeune; j'entends les bois retentir;
   Je suis jeune et jolie.

2 Trois jeunes fill'   vont y faner. (*bis*)
   Celle qu'accouch'   d'un nouveau-né.
   Je suis jeune; j'entends les bois retentir;
   Je suis jeune et jolie.

3 Celle qu'accouch'   d'un nouveau-né. (*bis*)
   D'un mouchoir blanc   l'a env'loppé;

4 D'un mouchoir blanc   l'a env'loppé; (*bis*)
   Dans la rivière   ell' l'a jeté.

5 Dans la rivière   ell' l'a jeté. (*bis*)
   L'enfant s'est mis   à lui parler.

234

6 L'enfant s'est mis   à lui parler. *(bis)*
  "Ma bonne mèr',   là vous péchez."

7 "Ma bonne mèr',   là vous péchez." *(bis)*
  —"Mais, mon enfant,   qui te l'a dit?"

8 —"Mais, mon enfant,   qui te l'a dit?" *(bis)*
  —"Ce sont trois ange'   du paradis.

9 —"Ce sont trois ange'   du paradis. *(bis)*
  L'un est tout blanc,   et l'autre gris;

10 L'un est tout blanc,   et l'autre gris; *(bis)*
   L'autre ressemble   à Jésus-Christ."

11 L'autre ressemble   à Jésus-Christ." *(bis)*
   —"Ah! revenez,   mon cher enfant."

12 —"Ah! revenez,   mon cher enfant." *(bis)*
   —Ma chère mère,   il n'est plus temps.

13 —"Ma chère mère   il n'est plus temps. *(bis)*
   Mon petit corps   s'en va calant;

14 Mon petit corps   s'en va calant; *(bis)*
   Mon petit cœur   s'en va mourant;

15 Mon petit cœur   s'en va mourant; *(bis)*
   Ma petite âme,   au paradis."

THE MIRACLE OF THE NEWBORN CHILD

1 They are three mowers in the field
  And in the field are mowers three,
  Three girls have come to turn the hay.
  I'm young, have an ear to hear the woodland revelry,
  I am young and fair to see.

2 Three girls have come to turn the hay,
  To turn the hay are maidens three,
  And one a mother's come to be.

235

3   And one a mother's come to be.
    A little babe, so young a maid—
    In kerchief white the baby laid.

4   In kerchief white the baby laid,
    The babe she laid in kerchief white,
    And into the sea by moonlight.

5   And into the sea by moonlight,
    By moonlight threw it into the sea.
    But the little babe said plaintively,

6   But the little babe said plaintively,
    Plaintively, without a tear,
    "You are sinning, mother dear.

7   "You are sinning, mother dear,
    Oh you are sinning, mother dear."
    "My child, my child, how did you hear?

8   "My child, my child, how did you hear,
    And who, my child, has told of me?"
    "In Paradise 'twas angels three.

9   "In Paradise 'twas angels three,
    Angels three and angels bright,
    The one was gray and one was white.

10 "The one was gray and one was white,
    Such angels have I seen above,
    And one did shine with Jesus' love.

11 "And one did shine with Jesus' love,
    The brightest of the angels three."
    "My child, my child, come back to me.

12 "My child, my child, come back to me,
    My little child, come here, come here."
    "It is too late, my mother dear.

13 "It is too late, my mother dear.
    The time has come and I must drown;
    My little body's sinking down.

14 "My little body's sinking down;
Too late, my mother, you are crying,
For my little heart is dying.

15 "For my little heart is dying,
For my little heart is dying,
And my little soul is flying."

Il S'est Mis à Turlutter

THERE WAS AN OLD GRANDMOTHER

C'é -tait u - ne vieill' grand'-mè - re, di - gue din - dai - ne, qui ne fai - sait que pleu - rer____, di - gue din - dé, qui ne fai - sait que pleu - rer, qui ne fai - sait que pleu - r - er.

Il S'est Mis à Turlutter

1 C'était une vieill' grand'mère,
   Digue dindaine,
      qui ne faisait que pleurer,
   Digue dindé,
      qui ne faisait que pleurer. (*bis*)

2 "Qu'à-vous donc, ma bonn' grand'mère,
   Digue dindaine
      qu'à-vous donc à tant pleurer?"
   Digue dindé,
      qu'à-vous donc à tant pleurer?" (*bis*)

3 "Je pleur' ton vieux grand-père . . .
      que les loups ont emmené.

4 Tous les moutons dans la plaine, . . .
      que les loups ont étranglé."

238

5 "Que donneriez-vous, grand'mère, . . .
  si j'allais vous les chercher?"

6 Il a pris sa turlanline, . . .
  il s'est mis à turlutter.

7 A vu venir le grand-père, . . .
  ses moutons a ramené.

8 Ils se sont pris par la patte, . . .
  ils se sont mis à danser.

THERE WAS AN OLD GRANDMOTHER

1 There was once an old grandmother,
  Digue dindaine,
  who sat weeping hour by hour,
  Digue dindé,
  who sat weeping hour by hour. (*bis*)

2 "Tell me why, my good grandmother, . . .
  you sit weeping hour by hour?"

3 "I lament your old grandfather, . . .
  whom the wolves by now devour.

4 And the sheep from our green meadow . . .
  that the wicked wolves have slain."

5 "What will you give, grandmother, . . .
  if I bring them back again?"

6 So he took his pipe and tootled . . .
  till the missing flock was found.

7 And the sheep and old grandfather . . .
  came to her safe and sound.

8 Then they took them by their trotters, . . .
  and danced a merry round.

À Saint-Malo

AT SAINT-MALO

A Saint-Ma - lo, beau port de mer, A Saint-Ma -
lo, beau port de mer, Trois gros na - vir's sont ar - ri -
vés. Nous i - rons sur l'eau, nous y prom - pro - me -
ner, Nous i - rons jou - er dans l'î - le, dans l'î - le.

À Saint-Malo

1 À Saint-Malo, beau port de mer, (*bis*)
Trois gros navirs's sont arrivés.
 Nous irons sur l'eau, nous y prom-promener,
 Nous irons jouer dans l'île, dans l'île.

2 Trois gros navir's sont arrivés, (*bis*)
Chargés d'avoine, chargés de blé.
 (*Refrain*)

3 Chargés d'avoine, chargés de blé. (*bis*)
Trois dam's s'en viennent les marchander.

4 Trois dam's s'en viennent les marchander. (*bis*)
"Marchand, marchand, combien ton blé?"

5 "Marchand, marchand, combien ton blé?" (*bis*)
—"Trois francs, l'avoine; six francs, le blé."

240

6 —"Trois francs, l'avoine;   six francs, le blé?"
—"C'est bien trop cher   d'un' bonn' moitié."

7 —"C'est bien trop cher   d'un' bonn' moitié." *(bis)*
—"Si j'le vends pas   j'le donnerai."

8 —"Si j'le vends pas   j'le donnerai." *(bis)*
—"A ce prix-là,   on va s'arranger."

AT SAINT-MALO

1 To Saint-Malo, port on the sea,
Did come a-sailing vessels three.
We're going to glide on the water, water, away,
On the isle, on the isle to play.

2 Did come a-sailing vessels fleet,
Laden with oats and laden with wheat.

3 Laden with wheat and laden with oats,
Three ladies came to bargain groats.

4 Three ladies came in the market street.
"Merchant, tell me the price of wheat.

5 "Merchant, tell me the price of your grain."
"Three francs for the oats, and little to gain.

6 "Six francs for the wheat, and the oats are three."
"And even the half's too dear for me.

7 "The grain's too dear by more than a half."
"If it will not sell, I'll give it like chaff.

8 "And I'll give it like chaff, if it will not sell."
"Why, then we'll come to terms right well."

L'Hirondelle, Messagère de L'Amour
THE SWALLOW, MESSENGER OF LOVE

Ah! toi, belle hi - ron-del - le, qui vole i - ci, N'as-tu
pas vu, dans ces î - les, mon A - lex - is, Qui est par -
ti dans les voy - a - ges, en ces longs jours? Il te don -
ne - ra des nou - vel - les de son re - tour.

L'Hirondelle, Messagère de l'Amour

1   "Ah! toi, belle hirondelle,   qui vole ici,
     N'as-tu pas vu, dans ces îles,   mon Alexis
     Qui est parti dans les voyages,   en ces longs jours?
     Il te donnera des nouvelles   de son retour."

2   L'oiseau qu'est tout aimable   s'est envolé.
     Avec son léger plumage   s'en est allé,
     A traversé l'eau et la mer   sans se lasser;
     Dessus les mats de cette flotte   s'est reposé.

3   A-t aperçu la hune   d'un bâtiment.
     Alexis s'y lamente   en naviguant.
     "Parle-moi donc, amant fidèle,   parle-moi donc!
     Je viens de la part de ta belle,   dans ces vallons."

4   L'amant plein de surprise   d'entendr' parler,
     De savoir des nouvelles   d' sa bien-aimé':

242

"Tu lui diras, belle hirondelle, qu'à mes amours
Je lui serai chaste et fidèle à mon retour."

5   L'oiseau qu'est tout aimable s'est envolé.
    Droit à son vert bocage a retourné.
    "Consolez-vous, charmante Hélène, consolez-vous!
    Car j'ai de si bonnes nouvelles qui sont pour vous:

6   "Votre amant sur la mer-e est engagé
    Pour faire un long voyage de douze anné's.
    Il m'a donné son cœur en gage et ses amours.
    Il vous sera chaste et fidèle à son retour."

7   "Adieu, charmante Hélène! nous faut partir.
    Le verre et la bouteille pour nous conduir'!
    Je te salu', charmante belle, salut à toi!
    Si ton petit cœur est en peine qu'il pri' pour moi!"

THE SWALLOW, MESSENGER OF LOVE

1   "O swallow, swallow, you that fly about and round,
    In far-off isles have you not my Alexis found?
    Now he is voyaging at sea, these weary days,
    And he must tell you of his soon returning ways."

2   The bird is sweetly willing and he takes his flight,
    Leaves all behind, away and away with feathers light;
    Never tiring, crosses waters and the sea,
    Till by a fleet of ships he settles warily.

3   Standing in the topmost rigging of a ship,
    Alexis sings complaint, the billows rise and dip.
    "Speak to me, O faithful lover, speak to me!
    From your beloved I have come away to sea."

4   The lover's taken all aback to hear the swallow speak,
    To hear of his beloved from the swallow's beak.
    "O tell her, swallow dear, that I shall faithful be
    To my beloved when I've come back from the sea."

243

5   The bird is sweetly willing and he takes his flight
Straight to his greenwood grove away with feathers light.
"O be consoled, charming Hélène, O be consoled!
Good news I bring for you, by sweet Alexis told.

6   "Your lover voyages about right busily,
He's taking twelve years for a voyage on the sea,
But he has taken oath of high fidelity
To his beloved when he's come back from the sea."

7   "Good-bye, charming Hélène! now I must leave you here!
Full glass and waning flask will guide us, never fear.
Charming Hélène, I bid you greeting! Hail to thee!
And if your little heart is grieved, O pray for me."

C'est l'Aviron Qui Nous Mène

COMING BACK HOME

M'en re-ve-nant de la jo-li' Ro-chel-le,

— J'ai ren-con-tré trois jo-li's de-moi-sell's. C'est l'a-vi-

ron qui nous mèn', qui nous mont', C'est l'av-i-ron qui nous monte en haut.

C'est l'Aviron Qui Nous Mène

1 M'en revenant   de la joli' Rochelle, (*bis*)
J'ai rencontré   trois joli's demoisell's.
C'est l'aviron qui nous mèn', qui nous mont',
C'est l'aviron qui nous monte en haut.

2 J'ai rencontré   trois jolies demoiselles. (*bis*)
N'ai pas choisi,   mais j'ai pris la plus bell'.

3 N'ai pas choisi,   mais j'ai pris la plus belle. (*bis*)
Je l'ai monté   avec moi sur la selle.

4 Je l'ai monté   avec moi sur la selle. (*bis*)
J'ai fait cent lieues   sans parler avec elle.

5 J'ai fait cent lieues   sans parler avec elle. (*bis*)
Après cent lieues,   ell' me demande à boire.

6 Après cent lieues,   ell' me demande à boire. (*bis*)
Je l'ai conduit   tout droit à la rivière.

7 Je l'ai conduit   tout droit à la rivière. (*bis*)
Quand elle y fut,   ell' ne voulut point boire.

245

8 Quand elle y fut,   ell' ne voulut point boire. *(bis)*
Je l'ai conduit   tout droit dessur son père.

9 Je l'ai conduit   tout droit dessur son père. *(bis)*
Quand ell' fut là,   ell' buvait à plein verre.

COMING BACK HOME

1 As I was coming back from fair Rochelle, O, *(bis)*
I came upon three pretty demoisell's.
It is the paddle that drives the canoe,
It is the paddle that moves us on.

2 I took away the prettiest of the three, *(bis)*
And mounted her upon my horse with me.

3 One hundred leagues in silence did we ride, O, *(bis)*
When suddenly, "I want a drink," she cried.

4 I led her quickly to the river's brink, O, *(bis)*
But when I got her there, she would not drink.

5 I took the damsel homeward by and by, O, *(bis)*
And then she drank and drained a beaker dry.

Je Sais Bien Quelque Chose

I KNOW A THING OR TWO

C'est en m'y pro — me — nant, le long de ces prai-
ri - es, Dans mon che-min ren - con - tre Mar-gue- ri - te, m'a -
mi———— e. Je sais bien quel - que cho se que je ne
veux pas di - re, Ah! Que je ne di - rai pas.

Je Sais Bien Quelque Chose

1 C'est en m'y promenant,   le long de ces prairies,
   Dans mon chemin rencontre   Marguerite, m'amie.
   Je sais bien quelque chose
   Que je ne veux pas dire,
   Ah!
   Que je ne dirai pas.

2 "Qu'avez-vous à soupirer,   Marguerite, m'amie?"
   "Ne sais-tu pas, galant,   que mon père m'y marie?

3 Ne sais-tu pas, galant,   que mon père m'y marie?
   A un vieillard bonhomm'   qui a la barbe grise?

4 Je voudrais que ces vieux   soient dedans un navire,
   A cinq cents lieues au larg',   sans pain et sans farine,

5 Pour leur montrer par là   pucelles à poursuivre.
   Les vieux sont pour les vieill's,   les garçons pour les filles."

247

1 As through the fields I walked   merry was I to meet her,
   She is the girl I fancy,   my Marguerite, none sweeter.
   I know a thing or two,
   A thing or two I do,
   But ah!
   I'll never tell it you.

2 "Tell me, my Marguerite, why weeping here you tarry?"
   "Do you not know that father tells me that I must marry?

3 I am to have a bridegroom   grizzled and weak and silly;
   Whether I want or no, I   must take him willy-nilly.

4 What a good thing 'twould be if   all these old men were taken
   Many miles out to sea to   starve and to die forsaken!

5 Let the old men have crones,   maidens they should not tether.
   Crabbèd old age and youth   never can live together."

Cette Aimable Tourterelle

THIS LOVELY TURTLEDOVE

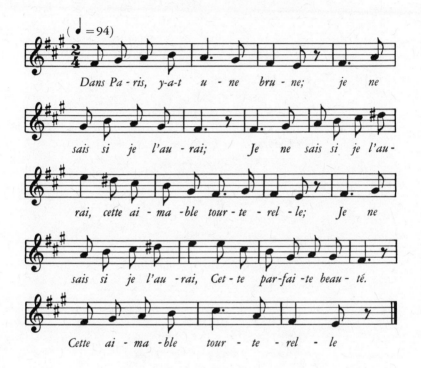

Dans Pa - ris, y-a-t u - ne bru - ne; je ne
sais si je l'au - rai; Je ne sais si je l'au -
rai, cette ai - ma - ble tour - te - rel - le; Je ne
sais si je l'au - rai, Cet - te par-fai -te beau - té.
Cette ai - ma - ble tour - te - rel - le

Cette Aimable Tourterelle

1 Dans Paris, y-a-t une brune; je ne sais si je l'aurai;
Je ne sais si je l'aurai, cette aimable tourterelle;
Je ne sais si je l'aurai,
Cette parfaite beauté.

2 Cette aimable tourterelle est toujours en me disant:
"Ah! que nous serions heureux d'être mari-és ensemble!
Ah! que nous serions heureux
D'être mari-és tous deux!"

249

3 —"Faisons nos promess's ensemble; n'attendons pas à demain."
Je lui présente la main; ell' me présente la rose.
   Ell' me dit en souri-ant:
   "Soyez mon fidèle amant!"

THIS LOVELY TURTLEDOVE

1 In Paris there's a little brunette,
    I know not if she's mine to be,
    I know not if she's mine to be,
    This lovely turtle-dovey-dovie;
    I know not if she's mine to be,
    This perfect little béauty.

2 This lovely turtledove, O she
    Is ever and ever telling me:
    "Oh, how happy we shall be,"
    And then she heaves a little sigh,
    "Oh, how happy we shall be
    When we are married, you and I!"

3 "Then let us promise each to each,
    Nor wait till comes the morrow day."
    I give my hand to turtledove,
    She gives me a rose, a rose away.
    And turtledove she smiles to me:
    "O be my lover faithfully!"

Je Ne Suis Pas Si Vilaine

I'M NOT QUITE OF PEASANTRY

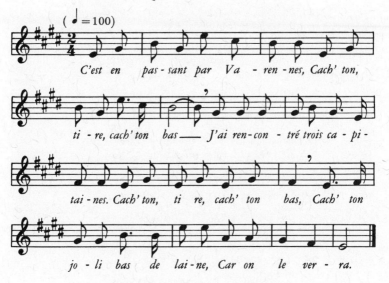

C'est en pas-sant par Va - ren-nes, Cach' ton,
ti - re, cach' ton bas___ J'ai ren-con - tré trois ca - pi -
tai - nes. Cach' ton, ti re, cach' ton bas, Cach' ton
jo - li bas de lai-ne, Car on le ver - ra.

Je Ne Suis Pas Si Vilaine

1 C'est en passant par Varennes,
  Cach' ton, tire, cach' ton bas,
  J'ai rencontré trois capitaines.
  Cach' ton, tire, cach' ton bas,
  Cach' ton joli bas de laine,
  Car on le verra.

2 J'ai rencontré trois capitaines.
  Cach' ton, tire, cach' ton bas,
  Ils m'ont traité de vilaine.
  Cach' ton, tire, cach' ton bas,
  Cach' ton joli bas de laine,
  Car on le verra.

3 Ils m'ont traité de vilaine.
  Je ne suis pas si vilaine,

4 Je ne suis pas si vilaine,
  Puisque le fils du roi m'aime.

5 Puisque le fils du roi m'aime.
  Il m'a donné pour étrennes

6 Il m'a donné pour étrennes
  Un beau violon d'ébène,

7 Un beau violon d'ébène,
  Une rose de marjolaine.

8 Une rose de marjolaine.
  Si ell' fleurit, je s'rai reine,

9 Si ell' fleurit, je s'rai reine,
  Si ell' flétrit, je s'rai vilaine.

251

I'M NOT QUITE OF PEASANTRY

1 By Varennes going carelessly,
   Hide your, dingle, hide your stocking,
   Captains coming I met three,
   Hide your, dingle, hide your stocking,
   Hide your pretty woolen stocking,
   People will be looking.

2 Captains coming I met three,
   As I were low-born spoke to me.

3 As I were low-born spoke to me,
   Yet I'm not quite of peasantry,

4 Yet I'm not quite of peasantry,
   For a kingly youth's in love with me.

5 For a kingly youth's in love with me,
   Has made me gifts of a holiday.

6 Has made me gifts of a holiday,
   A violin of ebony,

7 A violin of ebony,
   A rosebud beautiful to see,

8 A rosebud beautiful to see,
   And if it flowers, queen I'll be,

9 And if it flowers, queen I'll be,
   And if it fades, all peasantry.

L'Herbe Verdit Tous les Printemps

THE FLOWERS COME EVERY SPRING

Par un ma - tin —, au point du — jour, Par un matin ——, au point du —— jour, J'ai en - ten-
du chan - ter — l'a - mour Par un' tant jo - li' — pas - tou-
rel - le, Que tous les ber - gers — d'a - len - tours
Se sont ras - sem - blés — au -tour d'el - le.

L'Herbe Verdit Tous les Printemps

1   Par un matin, au point du jour, (*bis*)
J'ai entendu chanter l'amour
Par un' tant joli' pastourelle
Que tous les bergers d'alentours
Se sont rassemblés autour d'elle.

2   En voyant sa rare beauté, (*bis*)
D'elle je me suis approché.
Je me suis approché d'elle,
En lui disant: "Je suis berger.
Prends-moi pour ton amant fidèle!"

253

3 La belle répond d'un air doux: (*bis*)
"Petit badin, retirez-vous!
Moi, je suis pastourelle sage.
Si vous n'étiez pas si jaloux,
Je vous aimerais davantage."

4 "La bell', si j'ai perdu mon temps, (*bis*)
En cherchant bien, j'en trouv'rai autant,
Une autre que vous, aussi belle.
L'herbe verdit tous les printemps;
Les fleurs aux champs s'y renouvellent."

THE FLOWERS COME EVERY SPRING

1 Early one morning at dawning of day, (*bis*)
Such a song of love I heard upon my way
By a most entrancing shepherd maiden.
Then all the shepherds sang a roundelay,
Off'ring her their hands with flowers laden.

2 Viewing her beauty beyond all compare, (*bis*)
I drew near and told her, told her then and there,
"I pursue the shepherd's simple calling.
Pray give ear while I my passion true declare:
I adore you, shepherdess enthralling!"

3 Then my proud beauty did coyly reply, (*bis*)
"Sir, you waste your time, your suit I do deny;
Maids like me may not be treated lightly.
Were you not so jealous, peradventure I
Might agree to treat you more politely."

4 "Maiden, I'm wasting my time, I agree. (*bis*)
Many million fish are left in the sea;
I shall thrive despite your airs and graces.
What though ev'ry year the flowers faded be,
Next year other blooms will take their places."

About the Author

ELIZABETH YATES, author of over fifty books, a third of which are for children, is perhaps best known for her book *Amos Fortune, Free Man*, the winner of the 1951 Newbery Award. Carefully researched and convincingly written, it is a biography which displays a power of language and imagination that draws the reader into the life of an African prince who is enslaved and taken to America. As the steadfast hero painstakingly works his way to both spiritual and physical freedom, Miss Yates succeeds in making complex issues of injustice, fortitude and forgiveness remarkably accessible to the child. In *With Pipe, Paddle, and Song* she had a similar success in capturing for the thoughtful older child the reality and meaning of love between a man and a woman—a particularly challenging achievement in a day and age when love and relationship have been separated from their true context of commitment. A description about Elizabeth Yates, written by her husband William McGreal in 1951, reveals in part the reason for her success. He writes: "She has plenty of courage, a strong faith and a native expectancy of good. Living with her is a high adventure."

A life of adventure can begin quietly enough. Elizabeth Yates was born in New York State in 1905 and her first storymaking occurred on the back of her horse Bluemouse during long rides through the countryside. In 1926, still determined to be an author she moved to New York City to launch her writing career. She undertook a variety of assignments: reviewing books, writing short stories, and doing research. When she married William McGreal they moved to England where her first book, *High Holiday*, based on her travels in Switzerland with three English children, was published. In 1939 the McGreals returned to the United States and settled on an old farm in New Hampshire.

Miss Yates continued to write books, still finding time to pursue her other hobbies, which included gardening and walking. A friendship begun in England with artist Nora Unwin continued to flourish personally and professionally when, in 1946 the McGreals invited Miss Unwin to come to America to live. She eventually settled into a house on the McGreals' orchard. The artist and author collaborated on many projects, including *With Pipe, Paddle, and Song*, for which Miss Unwin did the front and back cover illustrations as well as the map at the beginning.

Miss Yates, now in her still vigorous nineties, lives in Concord, New Hampshire, continuing to live out her deep sense of faith and adventure in many ways. One of the things she does is to open her home to small groups of children to provide writing instruction and encouragement. One suspects that she shares with them this favorite verse:

> The written word should be
> Clean as a bone,
> Clear as light
> Hard as stone.
> Two words are not so good
> As one.